PRAISE for *What Do the Experts Say?*

"The timing of *What Do the Experts Say?* could not have been better. Just when certain factions of the reading research community and phonics-first ideologues are attempting to redefine what constitutes acceptable research and practice, Flippo's study is a welcomed breath of fresh air. The search for points of agreement among literacy experts with diverse beliefs and perspectives is what the literacy field should be engaged in, not derisive battles. This book is must reading for teachers, teacher educators, curriculum developers, policy makers, and state legislators who genuinely are concerned about children's literacy acquisition."

—Richard T. Vacca, President of International Reading Association (1996–1997), Professor of Education, Kent State University

"A thoughtful and revealing analysis of one of the most politicized and hotly debated topics in education today. The study reported in this book demonstrates that many of the opposing and conflicting views on reading instruction can come together to provide educators with a clear common message. As demonstrated in the descriptions of classroom instruction provided in this book, the best teachers make use of a variety of approaches and strategies to meet the diverse needs of their students. It should not be surprising to anyone that many of the findings from the Expert Study are consistent with findings from the National Assessment of Educational Progress regarding the relationship between instructional practice and reading achievement. With this work, Rona Flippo has demonstrated that it is possible to move beyond 'the great debate.' Moreover, she has provided us with a model for how to best support reading development—through skillful and reflective application of the best research in reading education."

—Jay R. Campbell, First Author of the 1994 National Assessment of Educational Progress (NAEP), Educational Testing Service

"Flippo argues that the lack of agreement among literacy teachers, scholars, and researchers about reading instruction has disempowered the literacy education community and has allowed noneducators to take control of framing policy and practice in reading education. The powerful message in this book should act as a wake-up call for those of us most closely connected with school reading instruction—reading teachers, reading teacher educators, and reading education researchers—to focus on our core and common beliefs so that our voices and our expertise, in advocacy for learners, will be heard beyond our own venues and into those places where decisions that affect the future of reading education will be made."

—Timothy Rasinski, Co-editor of *The Reading Teacher*, Professor of Education, Kent State University

"In this era of the reading wars waged between the phonics and whole language advocates, Rona Flippo's work is enlightening, encouraging, and absolutely necessary. She has not only delineated the common ground upon which the literacy experts can agree, but she has given us wonderful examples as to how that 'common ground' is implemented in classrooms around the country. *What Do the Experts Say? Helping Children Learn to Read* should be on the shelves of all reading professionals—classroom teachers, reading supervisors, and college educators."

—Jack Cassidy, President of the International Reading Association (1982–1983), Professor of Education, Texas A&M University-Corpus Christi

"What Do the Experts Say? finally provides educators with ideas and perspectives on reading instruction upon which the experts agree! Flippo's study helps to bridge the gap between several vastly different beliefs about what constitutes good literacy instruction. In today's political climate where education is at the forefront (particularly reading), the Expert Study lends a voice to the debate by defining instructional practices that consider children's motivation and development and are agreed upon by many highly respected and diverse reading experts. Not only does Flippo interview the experts, she also honors teachers' voices. As reading teachers in our school system, we gathered to read and discuss the Expert Study and we were all impressed by the thoughtful conversation her points provoked. Thank you for challenging our thinking about good literacy instruction!"

—Isabel Barrow, Director of Elementary Education, Greene County Schools, Virginia, and The Title I Teachers of Greene County Schools

"What do the experts say about reading instruction? Do our kids need a greater dose of phonics? Do they need to be immersed in whole language? Flippo's timely study sheds light on the controversies in the teaching of reading and presents some important expert agreements. Of particular note are the from-the-trenches comments in four chapters by classroom teachers. This book provides a balanced perspective on classroom reading practices and, for those who care, it provides points of consensus on which leading, but diverse reading experts do actually agree."

—Alden J. Moe, Co-author of the *Analytical Reading Inventory,* Professor of Education, Lehigh University

"In this day and age, with its seemingly endless debate over the most effective way to teach reading, be it phonics or whole language, or the basal reader, Rona Flippo's perspective in this volume is both refreshing and practical. Her research clearly shows that despite the differences of opinion on many of these issues in reading, there is a generally unrecognized common ground as well. This book is an important contribution to the field of reading education and should be read by all classroom teachers interested in becoming better reading teachers."

—Richard D. Robinson, Professor of Education, University of Missouri-Columbia

What Do the Experts Say?

| HELPING CHILDREN LEARN TO READ |

Rona F. Flippo

with chapters by contributing teachers

HEINEMANN

Portsmouth, NH

Heinemann
A division of Reed Elsevier Inc.
361 Hanover Street
Portsmouth, NH 03801–3912
http://www.heinemann.com

Offices and agents throughout the world

The author and publisher wish to thank those who have generously given permission to reprint borrowed material:

"I Had No Choice! Learning From the Experts" by Gay Fawcett includes material from "Beth Starts Like Brown Bear" by Gay Fawcett. Reprinted With Permission of Phi Delta Kappan (Volume 75, pp. 721–722, 1994).

Library of Congress Cataloging-in-Publication Data

Flippo, Rona F.
     What do the experts say?: helping children learn to read/Rona F. Flippo, with chapters by contributing teachers.
          p.   cm.
     Includes bibliographical references.
     ISBN 0-325-00044-1
     1. Reading (Elementary)   2. Children–Books and reading.
I. Title.
LB1573.F56   1999   98-54810
372.41–dc21   CIP

Editor: Lois Bridges
Production: Vicki Kasabian
Cover design: Michael Leary Design
Manufacturing: Louise Richardson

Printed in the United States of America on acid-free paper

03 02 01 00 99 DA 1 2 3 4 5

This book is dedicated to my family:

To my mother, Molly Fleig and my aunt, Anna Schmuckler, who have provided me with love and support throughout my entire life.

To my children, Tara Flippo and Todd Graham, who have provided me with love, support and grounding throughout my adult and professional life.

And last but not least, to my husband, Tyler Fox, who provides me with everything I need and who has been there for every presentation of this study and for most of "the debates."

Contents

Acknowledgments

I wish to acknowledge the contributions of the following people and to thank them for their help in making this book a reality. First and foremost, I thank Dick Anderson, Brian Cambourne, Ed Fry, Yetta Goodman, Jane Hansen, Jerry Harste, Wayne Otto, Scott Paris, David Pearson, George Spache, and Rand Spiro for their ongoing participation in "the expert study" throughout the ten *long* years it took to complete. They truly are "experts" in every sense of the word, and I am honored to have had the opportunity to work with each of them on this study. I also want to acknowledge Lois Bridges, my wonderful editor, for her foresight and perseverance in encouraging me to do this book *especially* for teachers and other school professionals.

Special thanks go to Jane Hansen, University of New Hampshire; Tim Rasinski, Kent State University; Vicki Risko, Peabody College of Vanderbilt University; and David Yaden, University of Southern California, who helped me locate the expert teachers who wrote chapters for this book.

The contributing teachers have been wonderful to work with, and they deserve special recognition and applause. Thank you so much for your contributions and wisdom: Gay Fawcett, Lilia Del Carmen Monzó, Kim Boothroyd, and Margaret Berry!

Jay Campbell of Educational Testing Service was extremely helpful to me as I planned and wrote the survey for the follow-up study located at the back of this book. Thank you, Jay, for sharing your expertise with me. Additionally, thanks are due to Gerry Coles, Dick Allington, and Julie Turner for their help with several pertinent citations.

I certainly would not want to forget the graduate students at Fitchburg State College, Sherri Borreson and Charlene Cormier, both of whom made important contributions and worked diligently on different aspects of this book; my excellent typist, Ron Elbert, for his expert typing and editorial assistance; nor the many classroom teachers who have taken graduate courses with me at Fitchburg State College. Throughout the years of data collection, as well as during the writing of this book, they helped me with their feedback not only on the study itself but on related manuscripts as well. Thank you all!

Introduction

If you are a teacher or school administrator reading this book, you are probably thinking, "What now? What will I be told I must do or not do this time?" Needless to say, you have probably been told what and how to teach and possibly admonished, too, for not doing it "the right way" more than once in your professional life. You have seen colleagues and other educators belittled by those who felt that they knew more than teachers and other school professionals. And at no time have you seen this more than in recent years during the so-called "Reading Wars."

You probably already know most of the arguments and have seen or heard how they've been used. In this book I will synthesize those arguments and present a study and the results that indicate that even though there are numerous differences in perspectives among reading "experts," some of whom have been pitted against each other by the media during the "Wars," they still do agree on some commonly held ideas and beliefs about contexts and practices for teaching reading in today's schools.

However, this book is *not* about how to teach reading. It does *not* attempt to suggest that any one method or approach is better or worse than any other. It doesn't presume to provide easy answers, because there aren't any. Instead, it has other purposes:

- first, to make clear a need for some agreements about reading;
- second, to report and discuss the agreements developed by those who participated in the study reported in this book;
- third, to give practicing teachers and school curriculum leaders an equal "voice" concerning beliefs, ideas, and learnings based on their classroom research and practices; and
- fourth, to suggest to you (the reader) that those of us in education must get the word out: We can agree on a good many things and these agreements should be made public so that the media and politicians will be aware of them as they shape and make school practices and policies.

To achieve these purposes I present in Chapter One an introduction to the problems in order to show the need for some agreements and common ground. Chapter Two reviews and describes "the Expert Study," telling about who the very diverse participating experts are and how the study was done. Chapter Three presents the agreements reached by "the experts"; then, in Chapter Four, I discuss and interpret the agreements. Next, four experienced and "expert" school practitioners discuss the findings from their vantage points in Chapters Five, Six, Seven, and Eight, sharing their views on how these findings fit into their classrooms, school situations, and experiences: Gay Fawcett, an Ohio curriculum director and experienced kindergarten, first and third grade teacher; Lilia Del Carmen Monzó, a California teacher of bilingual first, third, and fourth grade classrooms; Kim Boothroyd, a classroom teacher of preschool, first, second, and fourth grades in Seattle, New York City, and central New York state; and Margaret Berry, a first grade teacher in Nashville, Tennessee. Finally, I synthesize the study and the messages from the contributing teachers and practitioners in Chapter Nine and invite readers to participate in a follow-up study designed to give classroom teachers and other school professionals an equal "voice." (See the end of this book for a response form with full directions for participating.)

So we begin. As you read the chapters that follow, please keep notes of any questions, concerns, or other comments you might like to share. There is room on the response form for all of these, and your ideas are most welcome. Additionally, I really encourage you to take part in this follow-up study. Yes, of course, it is important to know what the experts say, but it is equally important to know what you as practicing teachers, administrators, and other experienced school professionals can agree to, what you believe, and why. Your voice is requested and *needed*, and rest assured I will see to it that your input is publicly shared. The time has come for teachers to enter the debate! Welcome and please step in!

1

An Introduction to the Problems

Establishing the Need
for Some Agreements and Common Ground

The general public has been royally led down the garden path by media and political sensationalism. They have been led to believe that their children have not been taught to read properly (blaming this on the whole language movement) and that large doses of phonics instruction are the panacea for all reading instruction situations for all children. These beliefs have resulted in more top-down control; legislation and mandates to teach and emphasize phonics; dictates on what materials to use and not use; diminished respect for classroom teachers and other literacy educators; and a de-emphasis on comprehension, comprehension strategies, and vocabulary/word knowledge (see Flippo 1997 for more details).

And, to make matters worse, the media have used experts representing different perspectives or philosophies, pitting them against each other (like prize cockfighters) in their various exposés (e.g., Collins 1997; Levine 1994, 1996; Shipley 1997) of what they love to dub the "Reading Wars" (Lemann 1997; Palmaffy 1997; Rubin 1997; Toch 1997). These public and orchestrated arguments (in major and local newspapers, and in most of the popular magazines) have effectively disempowered the experts involved—because they are deliberately positioned in these articles to have opposite views, they come across as agreeing on nothing and therefore their expertise is often "canceled out" in the eyes of the general public.

A Glimpse of What Has Been Going On

Take a look at some of these headlines that have appeared in national newspapers and magazines for a sense of what the public has been barraged with:

1

- "Reading Wars: Endless Squabbles Keep Kids From Getting the Help They Need" (*Chicago Tribune*, Rubin 1997)
- "Johnny Can Read If He Has the Right Instruction" (*Denver Post*, Athans 1998)
- "Parents Report on America's Reading Crisis: Why the Whole Language Approach to Teaching Has Failed Millions of Children" (*Parents Magazine*, Levine 1996)
- "Reading Methods Dividing Parish" (*Times-Picayune* [New Orleans], Shipley 1997)
- "Lost Generation of Readers Turn to Phonics for Help" (*Atlanta Journal Constitution*, Cumming 1998)
- "Maryland Panel Urges Increasing Teacher Training in Reading" (*Washington Post*, Valentine 1997)
- "State Report Urges Return to Basics in Teaching Reading Education: Panel Calls Progressive Methods a Failure That Could Doom Children Economically and Socially" (*Los Angeles Times*, Colvin 1995)
- "See Dick Flunk" (*Policy Review*, Palmaffy 1997) (Also see Flippo 1997 and 1998 for more!)

Is it any wonder that the general public has come to believe that their children are in jeopardy, that schools and teachers have failed their children, and that something must be done immediately? Is it any wonder that the general public also has come to believe that there are no agreements about the teaching of reading and therefore the authorities (usually the state departments of education and school boards) must step "in" and do something quick? Finally, is it any wonder that when the authorities have stepped in, they also believe that there are no agreements in the profession, and therefore have come up with their own "most expedient" ways of "doing something" (albeit mandating certain skills, methods, training, and materials). Certainly, they reason, "something" is better than nothing ("nothing" has been perceived as not making any drastic changes and just allowing teachers to teach according to their own perspectives and the children's needs and strategies).

So, in a nutshell, that is what we have been up against.

How and Where Did It All Begin?

The current momentum really began with test results that were inappropriately interpreted and used. When the 1994 National Assessment of Educational Progress (NAEP) data were released, they indicated that fourth-grade students in California's schools had tied for last place, along with Louisiana's, in reading achievement. California looked bad and politicians and school authorities in California looked at where to place the blame for their state's poor report. The "whole language philosophy" (inaccurately and repeatedly referred to in the media as a "method") became the target. California had been espousing use of a whole language method (really "philosophy") since 1987, when they adopted a literature-based language arts framework.

The California politicians and school authorities acted quickly to pass mandates requiring public schools to teach explicit phonics and spelling, use reading and skill basal programs that emphasize phonics instruction, and retrain teachers in phonics curriculum and materials. The media bought into it, publicizing the events and turmoil, and, of course, parents and other concerned citizens fell for it, too.

Passing the blame to whole language (rather than to existing and growing economic and sociocultural problems) went over so successfully in California that other states followed suit (North Carolina, Ohio, and Texas, to name just a few) and we now have all seen some of the results. More and more states continue to jump on the phonics focus bandwagon: Georgia, New York, Virginia, Washington and many, many others are part of this group. In fact, an informal ongoing survey, by the National Reading Conference (NRC) Legislative and Policy Committee 1998, indicated that out of the 34 states that had responded, 26 of them reported having proposed or enacted new legislation related to the teaching of reading in their public schools and colleges. (Readers might also want to see Flippo 1997, Manzo 1998, and Taylor 1998 for examples of what has been going on.)

What About the Data?
Didn't Students Look Bad in Phonics?

The NAEP data indicated nothing about students' competencies with phonics or phonemic awareness. Jay Campbell, first author of the 1994 NAEP, emphatically confirmed that the NAEP *did not* assess phonics skills, phonemic awareness, or other related graphophonic achievements (Campbell, part of symposium presented at CRA 1997). The NAEP data instead reported students' comprehension and the amount and kinds of reading they were doing in and out of school, with additional useful information pertinent to students' interests and motivations concerning reading.

For example, fourth-grade students were evaluated for their comprehension performance for literary and informative purposes and for reading habits. This included comprehension assessment using fiction and nonfiction materials (such as realistic fiction about animals, expository material on animals, fables, folk tales, and historical narratives). Students were tested to determine their explicit and implicit understandings gleaned from these materials by evaluating such skills as the ability to identify and make generalizations about character traits and motivations, locate specific facts, make comparisons, connect ideas and inferences, support interpretations, and recognize cause-effect relationships and authors' devices to convey information to readers. Additionally, students were questioned about the amount they read each day, reading for fun at home, and whether they discussed their readings at home. Use of the NAEP results to show a lack of competency in phonics is a huge leap that cannot be substantiated from NAEP data or from a review of the NAEP questions.

So Then What May Be the Reasons for Poor Performance?

In California, issues like the amount of dollars spent per student, the number of children per classroom, the overcrowding of schools, and the increasing number of ESL students and how they are being dealt with (note that by 1990, more than 137 different languages and cultures were represented in California's schools, California Commission on Teacher Credentialing, pp. 3–4) probably have more to do with poor performance than any particular philosophy, approaches, or methods the teachers may use or not use. California has by far the largest immigrant population in the United States; approximately one-quarter of California's population (about eight million) is foreign-born—a threefold increase since 1970, according to a census survey conducted in March 1996 (as reported in the *Los Angeles Times*, Knight 1997). A 1998 research report indicates correlatively that the number of poor young children in the U.S. over the last two decades can be attributed to the nation's three most populous states: California, Texas, and New York (Bennett and Li).

But these major problems in California were quickly brushed aside. Instead, the attack of the whole language method (philosophy) was much easier to deal with, especially when "phonics" seemed to be such an easy solution. (See Flippo 1997 for more, and McQuillan 1998 for his explanation of California's low NAEP scores.)

What Have Been the Outcomes?

In addition to the legislation, mandates, and top-down controls (for instance, state mandated phonics-based reading materials and programs, bills requiring phonics courses for preservice and inservice teachers, and other phonics-related "laws" which prescribe philosophy and instruction), we have seen a decrease in interest in the very important area actually tested by the NAEP: comprehension! "While politicians across the country are forcing teachers to focus on phonics and skills instruction, they are all but ignoring comprehension and vocabulary (word knowledge)" (Flippo 1997, 304). A study by Cassidy and Wenrich (1997) which focused on the current "hot" and "not hot" topics in reading research and practice indicated that the "hot" topics (meaning those receiving current, positive attention) are phonics, phonemic awareness, and skills instruction. "Not hot" topics (meaning those receiving negative or little attention) are comprehension, schema theory (important to comprehension), and word knowledge/vocabulary. A later study (Cassidy and Wenrich 1998) confirmed about the same results, but phonics went from "hot" to "very hot" and "schema theory" (again, important to understanding and comprehension) was so "not hot" that it was removed from the topics list!

Meanwhile, teachers, other school practitioners, administrators, curriculum leaders, and reading professors are being disenfranchised, disempowered, and disrespected. Their opinions are not requested or just ignored, and the classrooms, schools, programs, and research that they have devoted their professional lives to, are being destroyed or ignored. In the United States, many feel, we are moving backward rather than forward as politicians and school authorities tear down the many years of research and practice related to literacy development.

And it isn't over yet! In fact, as of this writing, the legislation, mandates, and other top-down controls are still emerging and seem actually to be increasing. For example, in addition to all the ongoing and developing state legislation regarding phonics (see "More States Moving to Make Phonics the Law," Manzo 1998), the federal government proposed The Reading Excellence Act, which would further restrict how reading is taught across the United States. And it looks as if these persistent interventions and attempts will continue for quite a while. (Lemann [1997, 134] predicts that efforts to establish greater quality control in public education, translating to "more central authority," will go on constantly over the next few decades, and politicians and the press will keep school curricula issues in the fore of American politics.) Only time will tell all the damages that have really occurred.

Finally, we have seen shock, outrage, and concern echoed throughout the reading profession (see, for instance, Allington 1997; Au 1997; Strickland 1998; Vacca 1996) and teaching profession (Routman 1996 and *The Reading Teacher* editorial by Rasinski, Pakak, and others 1998), and more and more discussions and planning are taking place to try to combat the problems and perceptions caused by the "Reading Wars" and the resulting "quick fix" panaceas that are popping up everywhere. For example, the various mandates to teach phonics have created the impression and expectation that if we simply change the focus of instruction to phonics or phonemic awareness, we will solve all children's potential reading problems. Efforts by the International

Reading Association (IRA), the National Council of Teachers of English (NCTE), and members of the literacy community have included increasing attempts to educate the media, politicians, and general public about beginning reading, the complexities of reading, and related areas. For instance:

- In 1997 the IRA published a position statement regarding the role of phonics in beginning instruction, stating that phonics instruction is important, but that it must be embedded in the context of a total reading/language arts program.
- In 1997 the NCTE passed their resolutions on phonics, basically indicating that phonics is only one part of the complex process of reading.
- IRA and NCTE, together with the Northwest Regional Laboratory, have co-published and promoted a book that focuses on core understandings about literacy learning and how children learn to read (Braunger and Lewis 1997).
- IRA has sponsored "Straight Talk About Beginning Reading Instruction" forums in various areas of the United States (for instance, see "IRA Forums Tackle Tough Topic" 1998).
- NCTE responded to the federally proposed Reading Excellence Act (1998), imploring people: "Urgent Action Needed! Children Who Are Learning to Read Today Need Your Help!"
- IRA passed a resolution in 1998 to indicate their opposition to the policy mandates that would restrict instructional practices, programs, materials, and assessments in classrooms, and that would narrowly define teacher education content knowledge requirements for pre- and inservice preparation of teachers.
- The IRA board issued a position statement in 1998 defining *phonemic awareness as "an understanding about spoken language,"* explaining the complex relationship between phonemic awareness and reading, and indicating that phonemic awareness (like *phonics, which they defined as "knowing the relationship between specific printed letters [including combinations of letters] and specific, spoken sounds"*) should not be overemphasized to the point that other important aspects of a balanced literacy curriculum are left out or abandoned.
- In 1998 the IRA and NCTE, together with other concerned professional organizations, founded the National Congress for Public Education for the purpose of bringing together diverse groups, including educators, policy makers, and representatives of the media, to talk about key educational issues.

But as excellent as these attempts are, and as excellent as are the persons involved in them, I believe something else is also needed.

What Do I Believe Could Also Help?

Announcements and shows of some agreements on the part of acknowledged experts in the field of reading would have some impact, in my opinion. It is also my belief that signs and announcements of agreement among experienced and practicing teachers and other school educators are equally important, and would have a telling effect.

Hence, "the Expert Study" (done with divergent and well-known reading experts) as described and presented in this book, followed up by a second study to be done with *you*, the experienced school educator, based on your responses after reading this book.

A public showing of some agreements among reading experts and professional school educators on "something" is clearly needed to convince the media, politicians, and general public that reading professors, teachers, school administrators, and other school professionals *know* what is important to reading development; know what they are doing; and know how to help *each* child develop his or her reading skills and strategies based on each child's needs and motivations. (This is not to say that any of us has all the answers. Of course we don't! We are still researching, learning and growing, but we have developed a certain amount of knowledge, expertise, and understanding about literacy development.) Without a showing of some agreements, we will all continue to be disempowered and disenfranchised from the literacy-related decisions in our classrooms and schools. I hope you will participate in this very necessary empowerment effort by participating in the planned follow-up study. (See the response form at the end of this book with full directions to ensure that your professional opinion is included.)

References

Allington, R.L. August/September 1997. "Overselling Phonics." *Reading Today* 15 (1): 15–16.

Athans, M. 1998. "Johnny Can Read If He Has the Right Instruction." *Denver Post,* 23 January, 17A–18A.

Au, K. 1997. "Constructivist Approaches, Phonics, and the Literacy Learning of Students of Diverse Backgrounds." Presidential Address, National Reading Conference, 47th Annual Meeting, Scottsdale, AZ, 4 December.

Bennett, N.G. and J. Li. 1998. "Early Childhood Poverty Research Brief 1: Young

Child Poverty in the States—Wide Variation and Significant Change." New York: National Center for Children in Poverty, Columbia University.

Braunger, J. and J.P. Lewis. 1997. *Building a Knowledge Base in Reading.* Portland, OR: Northwest Regional Educational Laboratory. Urbana, IL: National Council of Teachers of English. Newark, DE: International Reading Association.

California Commission on Teacher Credentialing. 1996. *Standards of Program Quality and Effectiveness for Professional Teacher Internship Programs for Multiple and Single-Subject Teaching Credentials with a (Bilingual) Crosscultural, Language, and Academic Development (CLAD/BCLAD) Emphasis.* Sacramento: California Commission on Teacher Credentialing.

Campbell, J.R. 1997. Comments made as part of the discussant panel for the general session "Finding Common Ground: A Review of the Expert Study." Rona F. Flippo, Keynote Speaker, College Reading Association, 41st Annual Conference, Boston, MA, 6 November.

Cassidy, J. and J.K. Wenrich. February/March 1997. "What's Hot, and What's Not for 1997." *Reading Today* 14 (4): 34.

———. February/March 1998. "What's Hot, and What's Not for 1998." *Reading Today* 15 (4): 1, 28.

Collins, J. 1997. "How Johnny Should Read." *Time,* 27 October, 78–81.

Colvin, R.L. 1995. "State Report Urges Return to Basics in Teaching Reading Education." *Los Angeles Times,* 13 September, A1.

Cumming, D. 1998. "Lost Generation of Readers Turn to Phonics for Help." *Atlanta Journal Constitution,* 1 February, A1.

Flippo, R.F. 1997. "Sensationalism, Politics, and Literacy: What's Going On?" *Phi Delta Kappan* 79 (4): 301–304.

———. 1998. "Points of Agreement: A Display of Professional Unity in Our Field." *The Reading Teacher* 52 (1): 30–40.

International Reading Association. May 1998. "Phonemic Awareness and the Teaching of Reading: A Position Statement of the International Reading Association." Newark, DE: International Reading Association.

———. May 1998. "Resolution on Policy Mandates." Newark, DE: International Reading Association.

———. January 1997. "The Role of Phonics in Reading Instruction: A Position Statement of the International Reading Association." Newark, DE: International Reading Association.

"IRA Forums Tackle Tough Topic." April/May 1998. *Reading Teacher* 15 (5): 1, 26.

Knight, H. 1997. "U.S. Immigrant Level at Highest Peak Since '30s." *Los Angeles Times,* 9 April, A1.

Lemann, N. 1997. "The Reading Wars." *Atlantic Monthly,* November, 128–130, 132–134.

Levine, A. 1994. "The Great Debate Revisited." *Atlantic Monthly,* December, 38–44.

_____ . 1996. "Parents Report on America's Reading Crisis: Why the Whole Language Approach to Teaching Has Failed Millions of Children." *Parents Magazine*, October, 63–68.

Manzo, K.K. April 29, 1998. "More States Moving to Make Phonics the Law." *Education Week* 17 (33): 24, 27.

McQuillan, J. 1998. *The Literacy Crisis: False Claims, Real Solutions.* Portsmouth, NH: Heinemann.

National Council of Teachers of English. November 1997. "On Phonics as a Part of Reading Instruction." Urbana, IL: National Council of Teachers of English.

NRC Legislative and Policy Committee. 1998. "Survey of States' Legislative Initiatives Related to Reading." Informal data compiled by the NRC Legislative and Policy Committee, May.

Palmaffy, T. 1997. "See Dick Flunk." *Policy Review*, November/December, 32–40.

Rasinski, T., N. Padak, et al. 1998. "Reading Wars . . . Nothing New." *The Reading Teacher* 51 (8): 630–631.

Routman, R. 1996. *Literacy at the Crossroads: Crucial Talk About Reading, Writing, and Other Teaching Dilemmas.* Portsmouth, NH: Heinemann.

Rubin, B.M. 1997. "Reading Wars: Endless Squabbles Keep Kids From Getting the Help They Need." *Chicago Tribune*, 2 March, section 2, 1, 4.

Shipley, S. 1997. "Reading Methods Dividing Parish." *Times-Picayune*, 19 April, B-1, B-3.

"Speak Out! NCTE Response to the Reading Excellence Act." 1998. Available from NCTE Website http://www.ncte.org/action/rea/speakout.html.

Strickland, D.S. June/July 1998. "Reading and the Media." *Reading Today* 15 (6): 12.

Taylor, D. 1998. *Beginning to Read and the Spin Doctors of Science.* Urbana, IL: National Council of Teachers of English.

Toch, T. 1997. "The Reading Wars Continue." *U.S. News and World Report*, 27 October, 77.

Vacca, R.T. October/November 1996. "The Reading Wars: Who Will Be the Winners? Who Will Be the Losers?" *Reading Today* 14 (2): 3.

Valentine, P.W. 1997. "Maryland Panel Urges Increasing Teacher Training in Reading." *Washington Post*, 10 December, B4.

2

"The Expert Study"

A Review of the Study, the Experts Involved, and the Procedure Used

By 1986, when I began this study, research on reading, writing, and learning was making a visible impact on how we all were thinking about instruction. For instance, we were aware of the importance of students' schemata as we planned for and introduced new concepts and topics (Anderson and Pearson 1984; Rumelhart 1980, 1984). We knew that reading and writing processes were interrelated (Langer 1986; Langer and Applebee 1986; Squire 1983; Stosky 1983). We knew that students should be given opportunities to read and respond to more "real" literature and texts for "real" purposes (Rosenblatt 1978). We knew that comprehension and developing metacognitive strategies (Baker and Brown 1984; Brown 1980; Palincsar and Brown 1984) were the ultimate goals of reading instruction. And, finally, we were aware that teaching skills and strategies could be done within the context of a reading or writing piece.

Even though we were all hearing, talking, and thinking about these ideas, there had been arguments and debates about their merits, as well as about the merits of other "new" ideas and perspectives, both at professional conferences and in the schools. As I attended conferences and visited schools, I became more and more curious about what we all did agree on regarding contexts and practices for instruction, particularly for reading instruction. Wouldn't it be helpful and interesting to sift that out? I thought, what if I asked recognized experts in the field of reading what they agreed with and I recorded their responses? Thus, the seed was planted, and I decided to do "the Expert Study."

How I Went About It

First, I decided I needed a starting place: a list of ideas or statements that I could ask well-known experts to respond to. I decided on Frank Smith's (1973) list of "Twelve Easy Ways to Make Learning to Read Difficult." When Smith published his list, he contended that if a teacher did any of the "things" on it, the children in the teacher's classroom would have difficulty learning to read.

Next, I brainstormed a list of names of acknowledged experts and researchers of reading who represented the broad and diverse range of research, beliefs, and perspectives regarding instruction. For me, this seemed to include a wide range of ideas as well as the three most prevalent perspectives: the traditional, whole language, and interactive. I sent each of these experts the list of "Twelve Easy Ways to Make Learning to Read Difficult" and asked them to respond by agreeing or disagreeing with each of Smith's statements. Also, if they were unsure, or if they questioned the wording of a statement, I asked them to so indicate. As you probably have guessed, not all the experts invited chose to participate. When I reviewed responses from those who did participate, moreover, I found that there was consensus on only three of the twelve Smith items. Even so, I was encouraged!

I compiled the shortened list of the names of experts who had participated in this first part of my study, and I decided that I needed validation to ensure that my "expert" list was actually representative of the diverse major perspectives. I asked P. David Pearson, who had recently edited and published the original *Handbook of Reading Research* (1984), in which he and others had surveyed and reviewed the entire field of reading, to review my list of participating experts. He did so and confirmed that, in his opinion, the list was balanced and representative of all the current major perspectives.

The Experts: Who Are They?

The names of the participating experts who would continue to participate for the entire study, along with a brief indication of what they are each most well-known for, are indicated for your information (also see Flippo 1997, 1998). Together they represent a wide and diverse range of ideas that include traditional, whole language, and interactive beliefs about reading instruction.

Although these experts would not want to be "labeled" in any simplistic way, the works that they are each most known for often do put them into one of the three main camps or positions: the *traditional* perspective, also known as the "text-based," "specific skills," or "bottom-up" perspective of how text is processed by readers; the *whole language* perspective, also known as the "reader-based," "holistic," or "top-down" perspective of how readers process text; and the *interactive* perspective, also known as the "integrated" perspective of text processing, which makes use of both text-based and reader-based processing (Flippo 1998). Since the media have often used these different positions as examples of "war" or at least of no agreements in the reading field, it is important to note that the experts in this study do represent both sides as well as the middle.

Richard Anderson is widely known as the lead author of the much-cited report *Becoming a Nation of Readers* (Anderson, Hiebert, Scott, and Wilkinson 1985) and for his extensive research on schemata, vocabulary, and children's reading.

Brian Cambourne, an Australian researcher and educator, is best known for his "Conditions of Learning" model discussed in *The Whole Story* (Cambourne 1988). The model is based on his study of learning environments in holistic classrooms. He has promoted the whole-language movement in Australia and in the United States.

Edward Fry is best known as the creator of "Fry's Readability Graph" (Fry 1977), the most widely used formula for determining the readability of textbooks. He is also an author of a supplemental basal reading program.

Yetta Goodman is the lead author of the *Reading Miscue Inventory* (Goodman, Watson, and Burke 1987), a well-known assessment tool for evaluating children's oral reading strategies. She has also developed other holistic observational and instructional strategies, and is a leader of the whole-language movement in the U.S. and worldwide.

Jane Hansen is (with Donald Graves) the creator of the "Author's Chair" (Graves and Hansen 1983), a well-known and widely used classroom strategy for highlighting the importance of authorship. She is particularly known for her work with reading and writing connections.

Jerry Harste is widely known for his research in early literacy and language development. He is one of the best-known advocates for the whole-language movement (e.g., see Harste, Woodward, and Burke 1984).

Wayne Otto is the creator of the "Wisconsin Design" (Otto 1977), a plan that was used nationwide for managing classroom reading instruction with a focus on specific skill development.

Scott Paris is widely known for his writing on authentic assessment and portfolio assessment (e.g., see Paris and Ayres 1994), as well as for the development of reading strategies.

P. David Pearson was the lead editor of the first *Handbook of Reading Research* (Pearson, Barr, Kamil, and Mosenthal 1984). He is widely known for his work in reading comprehension and for being co-director of the original "Standards Project for English Language Arts" (1992–1994). He is also an author of a basal reading program.

George Spache (deceased 1996) was the author of *Diagnostic Reading Scales* (Spache 1981), a widely used standardized reading test (first published in 1963). He is remembered for his research and leadership in the field of reading, and for being one of the early presidents of the International Reading Association as well as of the National Reading Conference.

Rand Spiro is particularly known for developing schema theoretic models of reading and for his related research on reading comprehension, text processing, and theories of cognitive flexibility (e.g., see Spiro, Coulson, Feltovich, and Anderson 1994).

What Came Next?

At this point I considered how I could proceed most effectively. Clearly, in order to find out what each of the experts could agree to, I needed more items for them to respond to. As I again reviewed their responses to the Smith items, I noted that various experts had questioned several of the items and made remarks or justifications next to these items. It occurred to me then that I could ask each of the individual experts to generate her or his own listings of "things" that would make learning to read difficult for students. And, conversely, what about asking them to also list "things" that in their individual opinions would "facilitate learning to read"? That is what I did!

Understanding the Research Procedure

I needed a process or procedure to efficiently and systematically gather the experts' ideas. I also needed a procedure to sift through the ideas generated and seek the agreement of each of the experts in my "panel." How would I be able to accomplish this? I wanted each expert to provide as many ideas as possible, and I wanted all of the other experts to review anonymously and accept or reject those ideas.

Using a Delphi technique, I found I was able to keep the process going. The Delphi is simply a means of structuring a group communication process in order to deal with a complex problem both efficiently and anonymously (Linstone and Turoff 1975). This allowed each member of my expert group to generate items (in this case, what they individually considered appropriate and inappropriate practices and contexts for reading instruction); and allowed the other group members to accept, reject, question, or edit the items.

Over a period of ten years, each of the experts generated items and sent them to me. I collated the suggested items from all of the experts, and then sent the complete lists to everyone on the expert panel. Each time, during each of the four rounds, the experts reviewed the items, indicated which they agreed with, which they disagreed with, which they questioned, and also at times edited items that they believed could stay on the list—but only with the included edits. Additionally, during each round, the experts generated new items for consideration.

After examining the responses from each round, items that more than two of the eleven experts disagreed with or that they questioned with a clearly understood rationale were dropped. (Remaining items that were questioned without any specific stated reason were followed up with a written or personal query to determine if the items should or should not be considered a disagreement.) Edited items were treated as new items, and they, along with the other newly generated items, were added to the bottom of the lists. All the remaining items and the newly generated items were reviewed during the next round. Therefore, throughout the process experts continually revisited previously accepted items, thereby further refining and sifting out the contexts and practices on which they could agree.

Why Is This Procedure Important, and Why Is It Important Who the Experts Are?

Very simply, if the experts are truly diverse, representing all sides of the so-called "phonics/whole language wars"; and if the procedure I used truly gave all the experts an opportunity to articulate their opinions regarding contexts and practices for reading instruction; then shouldn't we and others carefully consider their collective expert opinion?

At the conclusion of the data gathering, to further validate the diversity, representativeness, and balance of my expert participants, I asked an outside panel of six reading educators how they would categorize the experts involved in my study, based on the major work(s) for which each is most well known, and limiting the outside panel to the three prevalent perspectives previously described (traditional, whole language, and interactive). All of the outside panel members categorized the experts as I had, and all of them indicated that the group was diverse, representative, and balanced.

In the next chapter, the lists of agreements are presented for your scrutiny and reflection. Then, later, it will be your turn to give "voice" to your ideas.

References

Anderson, R.C. and P.D. Pearson. 1984. "A Schema-Theoretic View of Basic Processes in Reading Comprehension." In *Handbook of Reading Research*, ed. P.D. Pearson and section ed. R. Barr, M.L. Kamil, and P. Mosenthal, 255–291. New York: Longman.

Anderson, R.C., E.H. Hiebert, J.A. Scott, and I.G. Wilkinson. 1985. *Becoming a Nation of Readers*. Champaign, IL: Center for the Study of Reading.

Baker, L. and A. Brown. 1984. "Cognitive Monitoring in Reading." In *Understanding and Reading Comprehension,* ed. J. Flood, 21–44. Newark, DE: International Reading Association.

Brown, A.L. 1980. "Metacognitive Development and Reading." In *Theoretical Issues in Reading Comprehension,* ed. R.J. Spiro, B.C. Bruce, and W.F. Brewer, 453–481. Hillsdale, NJ: Lawrence Erlbaum Associates.

Cambourne, B. 1988. *The Whole Story.* Auckland, New Zealand: Ashton Scholastic.

Flippo, R.F. 1997. "Sensationalism, Politics, and Literacy: What's Going On?" *Phi Delta Kappan* 79 (4): 301–304.

_____. 1998. "Points of Agreement: A Display of Professional Unity in Our Field." *The Reading Teacher* 52 (1): 30–40.

Fry, E.B. 1977. "Fry's Readability Graph: Clarifications, Validity, and Extensions to Level 17." *Journal of Reading* 21 (3): 242–252.

Goodman, Y.M., D.J. Watson, and C.L. Burke. 1987. *Reading Miscue Inventory: Alternative Procedures.* New York: Richard C. Owen Publishers.

Graves, D. and J. Hansen. 1983. "The Author's Chair." *Language Arts* 60 (2): 176–183.

Harste, J.C., V.A. Woodward, and C.L. Burke. 1984. *Language Stories & Literacy Lessons.* Portsmouth, NH: Heinemann.

Langer, J.A. 1986. "Reading, Writing, and Understanding: An Analysis of the Construction of Meaning." *Written Communication* 3 (2): 219–267.

Langer, J.A. and A.N. Applebee. 1986. "Reading and Writing Instruction: Toward a Theory of Teaching and Learning." *Review of Research in Education,* ed. E.Z. Rothkopf, 171–194. Washington, DC: American Educational Research Association.

Linstone, H.A. and M. Turoff, ed. 1975. *The Delphi Method: Techniques and Applications.* Reading, MA: Addison-Wesley.

Otto, W. 1977. "The Wisconsin Design: A Reading Program for Individually Guided Education." In *Individually Guided Elementary Education: Concepts and Practices,* ed. H.J. Klausmeier, R.A. Rossmiller, and M. Saily, 137–149. New York: Academic Press.

Palincsar, A.S. and A. Brown. 1984. "Reciprocal Teaching of Comprehension-Fostering and Comprehension-Monitoring Activities." *Cognition and Instruction* 1:117–175.

Paris, S.G. and L.J. Ayres. 1994. *Becoming Reflective Students and Teachers with Portfolios and Authentic Assessment.* Washington, DC: American Psychological Association.

Pearson, P.D., ed., and R. Barr, M.L. Kamil, and P. Mosenthal, section ed. 1984. *Handbook of Reading Research.* New York: Longman.

Rosenblatt, L. 1978. *The Reader, the Text, the Poem: The Transactional Theory of the Literary Work.* Carbondale, IL: Southern Illinois University Press.

Rumelhart, D.E. 1980. "Schemata: The Building Blocks of Cognition." In *Theoretical Issues in Reading Comprehension,* ed. R.J. Spiro, B.C. Bruce, and W.F. Brewer, 35–58. Hillsdale, NJ: Lawrence Erlbaum Associates.

Rumelhart, D. 1984. "Understanding Understanding." In *Understanding Reading Comprehension*, ed. J. Flood, 1–20. Newark, DE: International Reading Association.

Smith, F. 1973. "Twelve Easy Ways to Make Learning to Read Difficult." In *Psycholinguistics and Reading*, ed. F. Smith, 183–196. New York: Holt, Rinehart, and Winston.

Spache, G.D. 1981. *Diagnostic Reading Scales: Revised Edition*. Monterey, CA: CTB/McGraw-Hill.

Spiro, R.J., R.L. Coulson, P.J. Feltovich, and D.K. Anderson. 1994. "Cognitive Flexibility Theory: Advanced Knowledge Acquisition in Ill-Structured Domains." In *Theoretical Models and Processes of Reading*, 4th ed., ed. R.B. Ruddell, M.R. Ruddell, and H. Singer, 602–615. Newark, DE: International Reading Association.

Squire, J. 1983. "Composing and Comprehending: Two Sides of the Same Basic Process." *Language Arts* 60 (5): 581–589.

Stosky, S. 1983. "Research on Reading/Writing Relationships: A Synthesis and Suggested Directions." *Language Arts* 60 (5): 627–642.

3

The Agreements
What Do the Experts Say?

So what did the experts actually agree on? After about ten years of generating items and reviewing and scrutinizing these items, the experts, it turned out, had agreed on a whole range of things. They agreed unanimously on thirty-three contexts and practices that would make learning to read difficult for children and another fifteen contexts and practices that they believed would facilitate learning to read!

There were also some other items that the experts "almost" agreed on, but because one or two of the eleven continued to question their wording, felt the need to qualify the items, or disagreed in some way with them, I have not included these "almost" agreements. However, all of the original "total agreement" items are listed here for your review.

Contexts and Practices That "Would Make Learning to Read Difficult": Original Total Agreements

1. Teach the children in your classroom letters and words one at a time, making sure each new letter or word is learned before moving on to the next letter or word.

2. Make word-perfect reading the prime objective of your classroom reading program.

3. Detect and correct all inappropriate or incorrect eye movements you observe as you watch children in your classroom during silent reading.

4. Emphasize only phonics instruction.

5. Make sure kids do it correctly or not at all.

6. Teach reading as something separate from writing, talking, and listening.

17

7. Give off expectations that reading is difficult and complex, and that "I really don't think you can do this."

8. Never let your pupils witness you enjoying/using reading.

9. Follow a basal without thinking.

10. Encourage competitive reading.

11. Use workbooks in every reading lesson.

12. Expect pupils to be able to spell all the words they can read.

13. Focus on skills rather than interpretation and comprehension.

14. If a child is not getting it, assign a few more skill sheets to remedy the problem.

15. Focus on the single best answer.

16. Make sure children understand the seriousness of falling behind.

17. Remove the freedom to make decisions about reading from the learner.

18. Group readers according to ability and let them know which group is the lowest.

19. Read infrequently to children.

20. Select all the stories children can read.

21. Stop reading aloud to children as soon as they get through the primer level.

22. Follow a basal series without questioning or reflecting on what you are doing.

23. Have kids read short, snappy texts rather than whole stories.

24. Make word-perfect oral reading the prime objective of your classroom reading program.

25. Have the children do oral reading exclusively.

26. In small groups, have children orally read a story, allowing one sentence or paragraph at a time for each child, and going around the group in either a clockwise or counter-clockwise rotation.

27. Drill children extensively on isolated letters and sounds using flashcards, the blackboard, or worksheets.

28. Test children with paper and pencil tests every time they complete a new story in their basal, and every time you have finished teaching a new skill.

29. Never give children books in which some of the words are unknown (i.e., words that you haven't previously taught or exposed them to in some way).

30. Be sure that you provide lots of training on all the reading skills prior to letting children read a story silently. Even if there isn't much time left for actual reading, you have to focus first on skill training.

31. Reading correctly or pronouncing words "exactly right" should be a prime objective of your classroom reading program.

32. Require children to write book reviews of every book they read.

33. Use flashcards to drill on isolated letter sounds.

Contexts and Practices That "Would Facilitate Learning to Read": Original Total Agreements

1. Develop positive self-perceptions and expectations.

2. Use every opportunity to bring reading/writing/ talking/ listening together so that each feeds off and feeds into the other.

3. Provide multiple, repeated demonstrations of how reading is done and/or used.

4. Organize your classroom around a variety of print settings, and use a variety of print settings in your classroom.

5. Focus on using reading as a tool for learning.

6. Use a broad spectrum of sources for student reading materials (i.e., children's literature, newspapers, magazines, etc.).

7. Combine reading and writing.

8. Make reading functional.

9. Include a variety of printed material and literature in your classroom so that students are exposed to numerous types of printed materials (i.e., newspapers, magazines, journals, textbooks, research books, trade books, library books, etc.).

10. Give your students lots of time and opportunity to read real books. Likewise, give your students lots of time and opportunity to write creatively and/or for purposeful school assignments.

11. Plan instruction and individual work so students engage in purposeful reading and writing most of the time rather than consciously separating reading from writing activities.

12. Create environments, contexts in which the children become convinced that reading does further the purposes of their lives.

13. Encourage children to talk about and share the different kinds of reading they do in a variety of ways with many others.

14. Use a range of functions of reading (print in the environment, magazines, newspapers, menus, directions, etc.).
15. Use silent reading whenever appropriate to the specific purpose.

Making the Agreement Lists More Useful

As I reviewed the total agreement items, I realized that in order to make them more useful to classroom teachers and other practitioners, I would need to eliminate or collapse many of the more redundant points of agreement from the original lists and edit them for clarity. The original list of contexts and practices that the experts totally agreed would "Make Learning to Read Difficult" would thus shrink from thirty-three to twenty-nine, and the number of nonredundant contexts and practices they unanimously agreed would "Facilitate Learning to Read" would fall similarly from fifteen to twelve (Flippo 1998). Additionally, it seemed to make sense to group the agreements into some clusters or natural categories that would help to organize and discuss them.

I reviewed, sorted, reviewed, and sorted some more, until I decided on five clusters which I have labeled "Combining Reading with Other Language Processes," "Contexts, Environment, and Purposes for Reading," "Developing (or Shaping) Students' Perceptions and Expectations," "Materials," and "Reading Instruction." Several of the agreements clearly fit into more than one cluster for me. When this was the case, I included them in as many clusters as I conceptualized them to fit. My choice of cluster categories and my arranging of the agreements into these categories are unique to my conceptualization and purpose. Others, of course, might choose other descriptors or cluster the items differently for their purposes. The experts subsequently approved all of my edits and groupings. They are presented in the section that follows.

The Clustered Summary Agreements

As you review these agreements it is important for you to keep in mind the "process" that I used to gather agreements from the diverse experts involved. Remember that they each generated listings of contexts and practices that they thought would make learning to read difficult and others that they believed would facilitate learning to read. Then they reviewed each other's suggestions, accepting, rejecting, questioning, or editing them. Because of this process, the product derived (the items on these lists) are not all equally significant or important to reading. Clearly, many of them are more important than others. Experts were not asked to rate their importance, as that would have complicated the process and the task. Additionally, for obvious reasons, the experts were not asked to come up with a list that was representative of "every" aspect of reading. Therefore, the agreements are not inclusive; they clearly do not represent every aspect or dimension of reading. However, these are the summary items on which all the experts (representing diverse perspectives) agreed, and they are important because they are the beginning of an opportunity for public announcements of some agreements in the field of reading education regarding contexts and practices for reading instruction in the classroom (Flippo 1998).

Contexts and Practices That "Would Make Learning to Read Difficult": Clustered Summary Agreements

Combining Reading with Other Language Processes

- Teach reading as something separate from writing, talking, and listening.
- Require children to write book reviews of every book they read.

Contexts, Environment, and Purposes for Reading

- Make sure kids do it correctly or not at all.
- Avoid reading for your own enjoyment or personal purposes in front of the students.
- Encourage competitive reading.
- Expect pupils to be able to spell all the words they can read.
- Focus on the single best answer.
- Make a practice of not reading aloud very often to children.
- Select all the stories that children read.
- Stop reading aloud to children as soon as they get through the primer level.
- Reading correctly or pronouncing words "exactly right" should be a prime objective of your classroom reading program.

Developing (or Shaping) Students' Perceptions and Expectations

- If students are weak in reading, let them know that reading is a difficult and complex process and that you do not expect them to be able to do the more difficult reading work.

- Avoid reading for your own enjoyment or personal purposes in front of the students.
- Expect pupils to be able to spell all the words they can read.
- Focus on the single best answer.
- Make sure children understand the seriousness of falling behind.
- Remove the freedom to make decisions about reading from the learner.

Materials

- Follow your basal's teaching procedures as detailed without making any modifications.
- Use workbooks with every reading lesson.
- If a child is not "getting it," assign a few more skill sheets to remedy the problem.
- Select all the stories that children read.
- Have kids read short, snappy texts rather than whole stories.
- Drill children on isolated letters and sounds using flashcards, chalk or magnetic boards, computers, or worksheets.
- Never give children books in which some of the words are unknown (i.e., words that you haven't previously taught or exposed them to in some way).

Reading Instruction

- Teach the children in your classroom letters and words one at a time, making sure each new letter or word is learned before moving on to the next letter or word.
- Detect and correct all inappropriate or incorrect eye movements you observe as you watch children in your classroom during silent reading.
- Emphasize only phonics instruction.
- Make sure kids do it correctly or not at all.
- Teach reading as something separate from writing, talking, and listening.
- Follow your basal reading program's teaching procedures as detailed without making any modifications.
- Use workbooks with every reading lesson.
- Focus on kids' learning the skills rather than on interpretation and comprehension.

- If a child is not getting it, assign a few more skill sheets to remedy the problem.
- Focus on the single best answer.
- Group readers according to ability.
- Have the children do oral reading exclusively.
- In small groups, have children orally read a story, allowing one sentence or paragraph at a time for each child, and going around the group in either a clockwise or counter-clockwise rotation.
- Drill children on isolated letters and sounds using flashcards, chalk or magnetic boards, computers, or worksheets.
- Test children with paper and pencil tests whenever they complete a new story in their basal, and each time you have finished teaching a new skill.
- Be sure that you provide lots of training on all the reading skills prior to letting children read a story silently. Even if there isn't much time left for actual reading, you have to focus first on skill training.
- Reading correctly or pronouncing words "exactly right" should be a prime objective of your classroom reading program.

Contexts and Practices That "Would Facilitate Learning to Read": Clustered Summary Agreements

Combining Reading with Other Language Processes

- Use every opportunity to bring reading/writing/talking/listening together so that each feeds off and feeds into the other.
- Instead of deliberately separating reading from writing, plan instruction and individual activities so that, most of the time, students engage in purposeful reading and writing.
- Encourage children to talk about and share the different kinds of reading they do in a variety of ways with many others.

Contexts, Environment, and Purposes for Reading

- Focus on using reading as a tool for learning.
- Make reading functional.
- Give your students lots of time and opportunity to read real books (both narrative and expository) as well as time and opportunity to

write creatively and for purposeful school assignments; e.g., to do research on a topic, to pursue an interest.

- Create environments, contexts in which the children become convinced that reading does further the purposes of their lives.
- Encourage children to talk about and share the different kinds of reading they do in a variety of ways with many others.
- Use silent reading whenever possible, if appropriate to the purpose.

Developing (or Shaping) Students' Perceptions and Expectations

- Develop positive self-perceptions and expectations.
- Create environments, contexts in which the children become convinced that reading does further the purposes of their lives.

Materials

- Use a broad spectrum of sources for student reading materials.
- Include a variety of printed material and literature in your classroom so that students are exposed to the different functions of numerous types of printed materials (e.g., newspapers, magazines, journals, textbooks, research books, trade books, library books, menus, directions).
- Give your students lots of time and opportunity to read real books (both narrative and expository) as well as to write creatively and for purposeful school assignments; e.g., to do research on a topic, to pursue an interest.

Reading Instruction

- Provide multiple, repeated demonstrations of how reading is done or used.
- Instead of deliberately separating reading from writing, plan instruction and individual activities so that, most of the time, students engage in purposeful reading and writing.
- Use silent reading whenever possible, if appropriate to the purpose.

So, What Does All of This Mean and Where Do We Go from Here?

This all means that diverse experts, from those with more traditional views to those with whole language views in the field of reading, including those who fall in between, do share some agreements regarding contexts and practices for reading instruction. Although they may "teach" differently, using many different methods and approaches to instruction with different children, they each do agree that certain contexts and practices tend to make learning to read difficult for children, and others tend to facilitate reading development. These agreements have been specified in this chapter. These same agreements will be reviewed, discussed, and interpreted in the next chapter. Later, you too will get the chance to respond to the agreements and see what you would agree on.

Reference

Flippo, R.F. 1998. "Points of Agreement: A Display of Professional Unity in Our Field." *The Reading Teacher* 52 (1): 30–40.

4

Discussion and Interpretation of the Findings
What Do We Know?

What do we know? We know a lot! First of all, we now know that experts from across diverse philosophies or perspectives are not in total disagreement. Instead they are actually in agreement regarding a number of contexts and practices for teaching reading! In fact, there are some contexts and practices that they unanimously believe would make learning to read unnecessarily difficult for children, and others that they unanimously believe would nurture or help children learn to read.

Secondly, we know from reviewing these agreements that reading experts from across perspectives, from those with more traditional views to those with whole language views, do not view the political solutions now being pushed as good for children and conducive to reading development. In fact, if you carefully review the agreements among these diverse experts, you will see that the political solutions offered from California as well as other states (e.g., North Carolina, Ohio, Texas, etc.) whose politicians are jumping on the "back to phonics" bandwagon are often just the opposite of what experts across a range of perspectives would agree with (Flippo 1997b).

Thirdly, we also know that these agreements *are not* about "how to teach reading." Reading development is far too complex to prescribe "how to" formulas to fit all children, teachers, and situations. Instead, we know that many different methods and approaches are desirable to meet the needs, strategies, and motivations of different children at different times and in different situations. Teachers must be given the professional latitude to select procedures, methods and approaches, and develop adaptations, that are appropriate for each particular child in each particular context (Flippo 1997b). Of course, teachers must understand the reading process, literacy development and the role of instruction in optimizing literacy development (Snow, Burns, and

Griffin 1998), as well as have a clear grasp and firm understanding of literacy and research learnings in order to make these instructional decisions (Pearson 1996). But legislatures won't achieve this by dictating procedures, approaches, and practices, in contexts with which most reading experts disagree (Flippo 1997b).

In the sections that follow, I summarize the experts' agreements from within each cluster, and then discuss and offer my interpretation of these findings. Next, I provide classroom portraits to illustrate how these agreements could play out in the context of actual classrooms when teachers employ these practices. To present and organize all of this, I use the following format in the succeeding pages:

- Clustered Agreement Category
- My Interpretation
- Illustrative Classroom Portraits

You might also want to refer back to the clustered summary lists in Chapter Three to review the agreement items for each cluster.

Combining Reading with Other Language Processes

The agreements in this category describe practices that involve how teachers use reading, writing, talking, and listening in their classrooms. Practices that experts believe "would make learning to read difficult" focus on teaching the language processes as very separate entities. Practices that experts believe "would facilitate learning to read" focus on combining use of all the language processes in teaching, particularly combining reading and writing, as well as talking about and sharing books and making all language instruction purposeful and meaningful to children.

It is clear that the experts agree that classroom reading instruction should not be separated from all the other language processes. Instead, they would like teachers to facilitate use of all language processes in their teaching, in meaningful ways for children. (Obviously, they do not see writing book reports on every book a child reads as meaningful.)

Other reports and reviews have revealed similar recommendations concerning the teaching of language processes. For instance, *Building a Knowledge Base in Reading*, a review of research co-published by the Northwest Regional Educational Laboratory, National Council of Teachers of English, and International Reading Association indicates that "reading and writing develop together" (pp. 30–31) and that "classroom experiences and instruction that integrate reading, writing, speaking, and listening support literacy development because they keep the language picture whole" (p. 64) (Braunger and Lewis 1997). *Preventing Reading Difficulties in Young Children* (Snow, Burns, and Griffin 1998), a recent report from the National Research Council, recommends that first through third grade curricula, to support the prevention of reading difficulties, include regular and frequent writing opportunities for children. And Tierney and Shanahan (1991) indicate that writing leads to improved reading achievement, reading leads to improved writing performance, and using a combination of reading and writing leads to further development in reading and writing.

So how does this translate into suggested classroom practices? What might this look like in a real primary grade classroom? I will give you my interpretation of what I believe the experts in this study would value, and then, through sample scenarios, provide you with a couple of classroom portraits to exemplify these ideas. Classroom teachers will no doubt find many more examples from their own "real" teaching.

My Interpretation

The experts value classroom contexts and practices that help children develop an awareness of the interrelatedness of written and oral communication *because these processes are so interrelated.* They also believe that children will become more fluent with these processes (reading, writing, talking, and listening) by using them often and in "real" and meaningful ways. The more fluent they become, the better they will get!

Certainly, we know that before children come to school they learn many things about language. Most of this learning comes from their real life situations, practice, and experiences rather than from segmented and contrived lessons. We know that we cannot duplicate in a classroom all the "real" experiences that could be associated with language processes; however, at the least, we can attempt to plan and integrate learning to simulate literate activities that could occur outside of school, making them as meaningful and plausible as possible for each of the children involved. The classroom teacher can design literacy learning situations and contexts to develop desirable outcomes like comfort with, and fluency and skill in, various reading, writing, speaking, and listening activities.

Mrs. Sullivan's Second-Grade Class

Mrs. Sullivan's class has been immersed in a study of fairy tales and fables. For a number of weeks children have been reading a wide variety of fairy tales, writing their own fairy tales, and sharing and discussing these tales. Additionally, children have been keeping journals with their own notations regarding the titles of fairy tales and fables they have read, their favorite plots and characters, and "author craft" words (e.g., "once upon a time," "a long time ago," "happily ever after," etc.). At the conclusion of the fairy tale and fable study, Mrs. Sullivan will have the children generate a listing of characteristics of fairy tales and fables based on their collective reading experience. Children will be encouraged to discuss and share from their notes and from the literature they have read and written examples of the characteristics that they and others generate. These characteristics will be displayed and referred to in the classroom.

Miss Garcia's First-Grade Class

Children in Miss Garcia's class have been learning about their community. This has included talking, sharing, reading, and writing about the roles of various community members (e.g., firefighters, police, doctors, teachers, students, priests, ministers, waiters, cable TV persons, recycling and garbage collection workers, etc.). Children's parents and/or family contacts and friends in these roles have been invited to the classroom to share their contributions to the community. Several children wrote invitations and others wrote thank-you notes to everyone who came. Miss Garcia has also carefully selected books and stories to read to the class about many of these community roles. The children developed a large mural depicting the community members they've read about, heard, or discussed. Together, Miss Garcia and the children have written a big book they call *Our Community*. All of the children have practiced reading *Our Community* and most of them are fluent. Miss Garcia lets children check it out overnight to bring home and read to their families. The boys and girls have made several other big books this year about other areas they have learned about with Miss Garcia. They are very proud of all the books they can now read.

Contexts, Environment, and Purposes for Reading

The agreements in this category describe classroom environments and contexts that set the stage for how reading is viewed in a classroom by the children. Practices that experts believe "would make learning to read difficult" focus on an environment that gives the message that word-perfect reading is the goal, correctness and being the best are the most important, reading for personal pleasure and sharing literature are a waste of time, and children's personal choices of literature are not to be valued. Practices that experts believe "would facilitate learning to read" focus on an environment that gives the message that reading can be useful to learning new things and can also

serve other purposes; there are many purposes for reading all types of literature; and books can be pleasurable and interesting to read, share, and discuss.

The experts clearly believe that the children's and teachers' views about
reading, children's motivations, and the overall classroom environment established by the teacher are very important. For example, if children get "the
message" that perfect oral reading is *the real goal*, then comprehension, reading for pleasure, and purposeful reading for information may not be seen as
important or as very valuable. Other research and reports have also indicated
the importance of students' motivations, the classroom environment, and the
importance of pleasurable, useful, and purposeful reading (Baumann and
Duffy 1997; Guthrie 1996, 1997; Pressley, Rankin, and Yokoi 1996).

Overall, research findings suggest among other things that effective
teachers endorse making literacy and literacy instruction motivating by establishing risk-free environments, providing positive feedback, conveying the
importance of reading/writing to real life purposes, encouraging an "I can
read" attitude, accepting children "where they are," conveying to children the
goals of lessons and why they are important, encouraging children to make
decisions about what they read, and encouraging self-selection of many materials based on children's personal interests and goals (Pressley, Rankin, and
Yokoi 1996). Experiences that provide students with opportunities for success, challenge, choice, and social collaboration promote motivation
(Gambrell, Palmer, and Codling 1993; Morrow 1996). It has become clear,
moreover, that children who are motivated and engaged with reading will
achieve in reading; while children who do not find reading as personally
meaningful can become disengaged, lose interest, and are more likely to show
less reading achievement (Guthrie 1997).

My Interpretation

Classroom environments and the contexts and purposes for reading that
teachers establish give children a message about what is important and what
is not so important. Eventually, children will "get" these messages and will
strive to do "good work" on what is considered important in those classrooms.
Conversely, they will pay less attention to skills, strategies, and purposes that
are not seen as particularly important or as valuable by the teacher. If it is important in a particular classroom to read for understanding, read for specific
information, read for pleasure, read many types of literature, and share and
discuss books that have been read and enjoyed, then children in that classroom
will value these things. On the other hand, if, in a particular classroom, perfect oral reading or getting "the correct" answer are what the teacher seems to
value the most, that is what children will aim for, whether or not a reading se-

lection has been understood, helpful, or pleasurable. We as teachers set the stage in our classrooms for what we will get by giving out "messages." We need to be sure that we give out messages that will reap what we truly believe will nurture and harvest reading and other literacy development.

Again, how might this translate into suggested classroom practice? What might this look like in a real primary grade classroom? Here are two classroom portraits that I believe would meet the approval of the experts. Again, these are only two of many possible examples. Classroom teachers will have many more from their own experience.

Mr. Robinson's Third-Grade Class

Children in this classroom are reading, sharing, and discussing various types of literature for most of the day. Some of this reading is assigned by Mr. Robinson for the class's current social studies or science projects, some of this reading is selected by various interest and cooperative groups that Mr. Robinson has established in the classroom, and some of this reading is selected individually by children during their free-reading time. Mr. Robinson provides equal time for the various reading purposes in his classroom.

For example, this week, for social studies, they are continuing to study transportation. Children are responsible for researching and reading about their cooperative group's preferred mode of transportation in one or more of the many nonfiction library books, encyclopedias, catalogues, and brochures Mr. Robinson has brought in. They can also use the Internet to supplement their research, and some groups will send e-mail to people involved with their mode of transportation to get more specific information. Each group has a list of questions that they must answer and they each have to cite their sources. The groups are required to report the information they found to the entire class and to lead class discussion about the type of transportation they have researched.

The special interest groups also have an assignment. They must read at least three selections from their group's preferred type of literature (e.g., fairy tales, books and stories about adventure, baseball, horses, etc.) and log them into their journals along with their personal comments. At the end of the month, just before it is time to switch into another special interest group, each group will be asked to share their favorite selections for the benefit of other students who might be looking for a good "horse" book.

Finally, all children are encouraged to read literature of their personal choice (e.g., books [fiction or nonfiction], stories, comics, magazines, newspapers, catalogues) each day. Mr. Robinson keeps a large selection of reading materials in the classroom, but children also are encouraged to go to the school library to select books; and they can bring reading materials, or other literature whenever they would like to, from home. Children can share these if they wish during a special time Mr. Robinson has set aside each day; but sharing isn't required if students prefer not to. Sometimes children read something that they just want to savor themselves, says Mr. Robinson. Mr. Robinson loves to read and wants the children to learn to appreciate reading, too. All reading is valued.

Mr. Robinson's classroom is one which makes it clear that reading for pleasure and for information are equally important, and the time allocated to share the pleasure and information derived is valuable time. Also, children who want to write their own books are encouraged to do so, and they can share these if they wish during the sharing time each day.

Mrs. Eckert's Kindergarten Class

Mrs. Eckert has been teaching kindergarten for a long time. She loves this age group and feels very privileged to have the opportunity to be most of the children's first *real* teacher. (She actually believes that children's parents/caregivers are their first teachers.) Because she believes so strongly in the importance of reading, she has nurtured an environment in her classroom to emphasize the pleasures and other benefits one can get from reading and sharing many good and interesting books. Children are literally immersed in books throughout the day.

For example, the day begins with Mrs. Eckert reading a special, carefully selected book to the children. She and the children talk about the book, and she encourages them to tell what they thought was so special or interesting or what they liked best about the book. Then she models what she thought was so special, interesting, and what she liked best. Children are then encouraged to bring up any special books that they have brought from home to share. They share what is special, interesting, and what they like about their books. As the day goes on, children are given plenty of time and opportunities to look at and "read" the many picture books and other books that Mrs. Eckert keeps in the classroom. Whenever possible, Mrs. Eckert has "rug times" to rest and relax while she reads other good special books. She is careful to choose nonfiction as well as fiction books to read to the children. She has noticed that the children are equally enraptured by well-illustrated nonfiction books about things that they are interested in, as well as literature from various genres. So she uses this knowledge to read and discuss a wide variety of literature with the children.

Additionally, Mrs. Eckert keeps *a lot* of paper, crayons, marking pens, and pencils available for the children to write and illustrate their own books.

She encourages this, and children share and *read* the books they *write* with her and with interested groups of their peers.

The children seem to love this special book environment. In fact, Mrs. Eckert indicates that they often say things to her like, "Have I got an interesting book for you today!" and "This one is very special. Let's read it together and enjoy. OK?"

Developing (or Shaping) Students' Perceptions and Expectations

The agreements in this category describe classroom practice that would tend to shape how children view themselves as readers. Classroom rules or ideas that experts believe "would make learning to read difficult" focus on practices that would lead some students to consider themselves as poor readers or non-readers who are not capable of successful reading, or of selecting their own books, and are not capable of spelling words correctly; and practices that would give a child the message that if he doesn't get it "correct" or if it takes him longer to do it, he is a failure. Classroom rules or ideas that experts believe "would facilitate learning to read" focus on practices that would help children develop positive self-perceptions and expectations of themselves, leading children to see that reading can be enjoyable for them as well as help them further the purposes of their lives.

The experts agree that it is important for children to value themselves as capable, successful readers. Students' self-perceptions are very important. Additionally, their self-perceptions lead to their expectations for themselves as readers and learners. Classroom contexts and practices that help children shape positive self-images about their reading abilities, choices, and performances are encouraged. Certainly practices that would lead a child to feel he can't do it right, he is too slow, or he is a failure are anti-productive to reading development.

Research does support the experts' agreements. For example, see the research reported in the previous section concerned with motivation (in particular note that Pressley et al. [1996] found that teachers who were considered "effective" reported that they encourage an "I can read" attitude in their classrooms). A study reported by Gambrell, Palmer, Codling, and Mazzoni (1996) revealed that students' self-concepts as readers are linked to their reading achievement. They also found that significant numbers of children do not view themselves as competent readers and are embarrassed by their own reading. Additionally, Oakes (1992) found that children labeled as "low" readers have low self-concepts.

My Interpretation

Classroom contexts and practices that refrain from labeling children as slow, low, or not capable, and instead build children's self-esteem as successful readers and writers are suggested. Labeling children often leads to defining and exaggerating what they cannot do. If we want them instead to be accomplished readers and writers, we need to highlight and emphasize what they can do. Classroom teachers are encouraged to use classroom organizations, structures, and contexts that make students want to read and write and be successful at it because reading is perceived as a useful, enjoyable, and successful endeavor and they are getting better and better at it all the time.

Here are two classroom portraits that I believe illustrate the experts' agreements in this cluster. Classroom teachers responding to this book are asked to consider sharing their own classroom portraits for future examples.

Ms. Valdez's First-Grade Class

Ms. Valdez's students are from many diverse cultures and represent several different home languages. She teaches in an inner-city school without much support staff. In other ways, the children in her classroom are fairly typical of first graders. For example, some of them are already "reading" real books, while others do not seem to read at all. Some of them can recognize, recite, and write many letters of the alphabet; others can't. Some of them are "writing" using invented spellings; others don't.

Ms. Valdez knows that it is important to help all children develop good self-perceptions about themselves as readers, writers, and learners. Because she believes in this so strongly, she works hard to encourage successful and enjoyable experiences for all children. She spends a lot of time reading to the children; she also spends a lot of time doing language experience dictation activities with children, encouraging them to learn new sight vocabulary words, writing books with them, modeling the reading of picture books and letting the children model them back when they want to, reading repetitive phrase books to and with children, and allowing them to read these books back to her.

Children who are already reading books with words share books that they have read or written. Children newer to reading share picture books, repetitive phrase books that they have learned, or books that they have written with Ms. Valdez. All children's reading and writing attempts are encouraged and valued. Children keep word cards for all the words that they know. Children can bring home books that they have read or written to share with their families. Ms. Valdez tells the boys and girls how proud she is of their reading accomplishments, and she means it!

Miss Mangiola's Second-Grade Class

Children in Miss Mangiola's classroom all keep portfolios of their reading and writing accomplishments. Miss Mangiola encourages the children to review their reading and writing "work folders" each week and select a sample to show something special that they learned, read, or wrote to place in their "portfolio of accomplishments." Children sometimes select the name of a book or a writing piece or other assignment associated with their reading selections for the week. Some children instead write in a word or two that they have learned that week. One boy put in his new public library card, which he had just gotten.

Many children in this classroom are keeping electronic rather than paper portfolios. These children are using a software program that allows them to design their own portfolios. Once they have selected representative samples from their week's work, they scan them into their portfolios, leaving space to type comments.

Children are all asked to reflect on their reading and writing accomplishments for the week and write an evaluation to go in their paper or electronic portfolios. Miss Mangiola is very proud of the children's development and accomplishments, and she lets each child know how proud she is each time they meet with her to share their portfolio samples and evaluations. Miss Mangiola also usually highlights these achievements by paraphrasing the accomplishments children share and by pointing out other positive learnings and strategies she has noted. Sometimes children ask Miss Mangiola to write or type her ideas about the work into their portfolios.

During parent/family conference meetings, Miss Mangiola asks permission of each child to allow her to share his or her "portfolio of accomplishments." Whenever possible, the child is invited to take part in the conference and show and explain his own accomplishments. Miss Mangiola often paraphrases and highlights the significance of the child's accomplishments for the family. If children want, they have their parents write or type their comments about the portfolio work. Children with electronic portfolios can print a copy of the whole or a part of the portfolio for their families to take home.

Materials

The agreements in this category describe the use of various materials for reading and other language processes in the classroom. Practices that experts believe "would make learning to read difficult" focus on using workbooks with all reading lessons, using the basal series slavishly and "no matter what," assigning skill sheets whenever children need assistance, using flashcards to drill on isolated letter sounds, removing the freedom to self-select stories and literature from the children, focusing on reading short paragraphs rather than reading whole stories, and only allowing children to read books after the teacher has taught all of the words. Practices that experts believe "would facilitate learning to read" focus on using a broad array of genres, and providing children with lots of time and opportunity to read real books, and to read and write for real purposes and interests.

Clearly the experts value the use of real and varied literature for instructional purposes rather than a frequent overuse of contrived materials, worksheets, and short out-of-context paragraphs. The experts have all agreed that using and following a commercially prepared basal program "slavishly" on a day-to-day basis is not a good idea. Nor do they recommend drilling children on isolated sounds or holding children back from reading a book until the teacher has taught all of the words. Finally, they have clearly emphasized that children should be given lots of time and opportunity to read and write for real purposes and interests, rather than for more contrived purposes.

Again, research reviews done by others confirm the experts' agreements. Adams (1990), for example, indicates that phonics is best learned in the context of connected, informative, engaging text; and that learning sight words in context seems to work better than learning them in isolation. Delpit (1988) endorses explicit instruction for children within meaningful contexts. Furthermore, Nicholson (1991) found that children read words better within a familiar context, like stories, than in isolation; and Purcell-Gates, McIntyre, and Freppon (1995) also found that contextualizing literacy experiences is beneficial.

Research by Simmons and Ammon (1989) indicates that when texts are rewritten to conform to grade-level standards or to a readability formula, as in the more contrived basals and reading materials, they can be more difficult for children to read. Cunningham (1990) indicates that worksheets and rote drills *are not* the best means of developing phonics. Finally, Braunger and Lewis (1997) emphasize that "what is critical is that children do read—lots, for sustained periods of time, for meaning, and for real and authentic purposes" (p. 54).

My Interpretation

The experts do not suggest that teachers *never* use contrived or commercial materials. In fact, I am fairly sure that most of them believe that there are circumstances and situations when use of these materials may be very appropriate and even necessary; additionally, some of them would advocate for use of a good basal program, which contained real literature, as long as the teachers who used them did not use them "slavishly." Readers of this book should remember, accordingly, that the experts' agreements *are not meant to be absolutes*. They are instead agreements, across perspectives, about what kinds of contexts and practices would tend to make learning to read difficult, and what would tend to facilitate learning to read for children. However, the experts *do* value the use of real and varied literature for reading instruction, and they *do* believe that whenever possible teachers should try to use real books and literature for their reading and other literacy-related instruction and development.

Obviously, too, the experts were also considering other issues when they reached these agreements which I have clustered under "Materials." The experts know, for instance, that children's motivations and interests have profound effects on their comprehension (Guthrie 1996, 1997; Tobias 1994). Certainly, children would be more motivated and more interested in self-selecting and reading real books and literature for real purposes, than in doing countless workbooks, skill sheets, and other drill materials much of the time. Certainly, too, children whose teachers use a basal "slavishly" day after day "no matter what" would probably get "turned off" to reading.

Two classroom portraits follow which I believe illustrate contexts and practices for using reading materials that the experts would approve of.

Miss Singh's Second-Grade Class

Miss Singh's school system has recently adopted a new basal program. All of the teachers in her school are being "strongly encouraged" to use it as a basis for their classroom reading instruction. Miss Singh did carefully review the new basal and was delighted to see that it contains a wonderful array of children's literature. Full stories, poems, and other genres are prevalent. The books are inviting, colorful, and she believes they would be attractive to children. There are also workbooks, skill sheets, and other commercially prepared materials to go with the program if she needs them.

Miss Singh has decided to use the basal, but *not* slavishly. She and the children will pick and choose from the stories and other selections offered in the basal. She will use the teacher's edition judiciously and as a resource to ideas to make the literature more meaningful for the children. She will only assign workbook pages and skillsheets when she thinks they are needed or would be really helpful for a particular child. She will also still allow plenty of classroom time each day for children to read real books of their own choosing and to write for real purposes and interests. She has decided that she will use this basal to its *real* advantage, as an anthology of good age-appropriate children's literature and as a resource to her (the teacher) for skill and strategy development instruction ideas within the context of each piece. But she will not limit her classroom literacy instruction efforts to just this one material. She is determined that there still will be many other reading choices and options for children in her classroom.

Mrs. Hughes's First-Grade Class

Mrs. Hughes is in a school system that has begun to emphasize skills instruction. They, like many other school systems, fear that children will not "get the skills" unless they are explicitly taught. Mrs. Hughes really doesn't disagree with that idea; she is also a believer in explicit instruction. However, she knows that she should try to use real, whole books and selections from a variety of genres whenever possible for her classroom reading materials. She also knows that whenever possible, she should let the children self-select many of their books and give them lots of time and opportunity to read and write according to their own purposes and interests. She doesn't want to turn them off to reading or to the enjoyment of literature.

Mrs. Hughes has reasoned that she can do all of this and still teach explicit reading skills. She plans to do her skills instruction whenever possible within the context of some of the literature she and the children read and discuss together. She feels certain that word recognition and other skills instruction doesn't have to be done in isolation, and that she can systematically teach all the required skills without forsaking the children's enjoyment of real books and literature. She knows she has to be careful, though, not to interrupt a good story just to point out all the words that begin with the consonant "b." Therefore, when necessary, she is willing to use commercially prepared materials for some of her skills instruction, but she is determined to do it in a way that will not turn children off. She feels that if children understand the reason for doing a particular worksheet and how learning "that" particular skill can be useful to them with their real reading pursuits, children will be cooperative. She also believes that children might even consider some of the skill practice sheets as fun or challenging, as long as she doesn't overdo it or make it *too* routine.

Reading Instruction

The agreements in this category describe a range of teaching practices that teachers may choose to use in their classrooms. The practices that experts believe "would make learning to read difficult" focus on teaching letters, sounds, and words in isolation; making word-perfect reading a prime objective; focusing on oral reading; doing round-robin reading; emphasizing only phonics instruction; emphasizing "getting it right"; teaching reading as separate from the other language processes; excessive use of workbooks; focusing on skills and using skill sheets excessively; using a basal without modification;

ability grouping; and requiring kids to take tests after every skill taught or story read. The practices that experts believe "would facilitate learning to read" focus on providing multiple demonstrations of how reading is done and used; using silent reading whenever appropriate; and planning the instruction so that students engage in purposeful reading and writing as part of the activity and their individual follow-up work.

The experts have come to agreement regarding a number of practices that they believe would not be conducive to reading, and far fewer practices that they believe would facilitate reading development. Obviously, overall, they are encouraging teachers to make reading and writing work and activities meaningful and purposeful for children, and to refrain from isolating instruction as much as possible from real text.

However, because these agreements, which are clustered under this category, also touch on so many issues related to reading, they are discussed in the paragraphs that follow.

Teaching letters, sounds, and words in isolation is generally not considered a good idea. Again, the preferred way is to call attention to and teach letters, sounds, and words within the context of real reading. Support for contextualizing this instruction can be found elsewhere as well. For example, based on their review of research, Snow et al. (1998) recommend language and literacy growth activities for pre-schoolers, in an integrated rather than an isolated fashion, to promote such areas as vocabulary development and the phonological structure of spoken words (pp. 320–321). Moustafa (1997) indicates that the optimum way to help children use their knowledge of spoken sounds to figure out unfamiliar print words is to help them learn to recognize print words in context (p. 56).

Additionally, Nagy and Herman (1985) assert that the major limitation of any approach that focuses on words *one at a time* is that it can only cover a small fraction of the words that students should be learning. Furthermore, Nagy, Herman, and Anderson's research (1985) indicates that acquiring vocabulary through reading (vocabulary learned in context) is considerably more (about ten times more) efficient (as determined by the number of words learned per minute) than direct vocabulary instruction by a teacher. Basically, they show that there are just too many words for anyone to learn them one at a time!

Focusing on children's oral reading is not a good idea either. When children are made to focus on their own oral reading "performance," they will pay less attention to the meaning of what they are reading. Additionally, as pointed out earlier, when the teacher seems to be focusing on oral reading performance, children get the "message" that pronouncing words correctly is the most important thing, and that other "things" like comprehension, strategies used, and information gleaned from the content are not as important. Other research and reports support this.

Samuels (1988) explains, for instance, that if children are devoting too much effort to sounding out words, they will not be able to direct enough of their attention to comprehension. Evans and Carr's research study (1985) showed that of the various teacher-led activities, oral reading of text had a *far lower* correlation with comprehension than did silent reading of text. Finally, Wilkinson and Anderson (1992) identified factors that make silent reading more efficient than reading aloud. For example, their research showed that during group oral reading time, there are many interruptions with other children calling out and oral errors being corrected. These interruptions interfere with children's engagement and comprehension. Additionally, the focus on performance, saying the words aloud for an audience, takes attention away from gaining meaning from the printed page.

The practice of "round-robin" reading is inappropriate for similar reasons. Again, the idea of having children read sentences or paragraphs aloud, one child following the other, as they each take a turn, going around the reading group circle, focuses on oral reading. And, to make matters even worse, children can predict when they will have their turn. Not surprisingly, before "a performance" in the presence of one's peers, most children will look ahead in order to rehearse as others are taking their turns to read. Of course, because most children are rehearsing, while one child does the oral reading, no one is really concerned with meaning, and everyone's comprehension is neglected.

Criticisms of the practice of round-robin reading are not new (see Allington 1980; Taubenheim and Christensen 1978; Taylor and Connor 1982). Overall, this practice interferes with comprehension development because the focus of round-robin reading is on correctly pronouncing words. Hoffman (1981) indicated that this is particularly the situation for less-abled readers. Finally, Johnston (1997) suggests that oral reading as part of a classroom round-robin activity "can be a socially threatening situation for readers who struggle with word recognition" (p. 193). Clearly, there is little, if any, support for this practice among reading researchers; and Pressley, Rankin, and Yokoi (1996), in their survey of primary teachers who had been nominated as effective, found that those teachers reported using round-robin reading "rarely" (p. 373).

The experts are not against phonics instruction; however, all of them, from more traditional perspectives through whole language perspectives, do not believe that emphasizing *only* phonics instruction is a good idea. Phonics is just one part of the instruction children need for word recognition development (IRA 1997; NCTE 1997). Additionally, phonics and other word recognition instruction are not enough. Children also need instruction for vocabulary, comprehension, and strategy development, which are *at the very least* as important as phonics and other word recognition instruction. Therefore, emphasizing phonics instruction alone is not recommended (Adams 1990; IRA 1997; NCTE 1997; Snow, Burns, and Griffin 1998).

In fact, Adams (1990), considered by many to be one of the most well-known researchers and proponents of phonics instruction, indicates: "However critical letter-to-sound correspondences may be, they are not enough. To become skillful readers, children need much more (p. 29) . . . phonics without connected reading amounts to useless mechanics" (p. 286). Additionally, Snow and her colleagues (1998) conclude in their review of research funded by the U.S. Department of Education that instruction in reading needs to focus on *both* word recognition and comprehension (p. 322).

Emphasizing "getting the right" answer or doing things "right" can lead children to make assumptions such as there is only one way to do something, "getting it right" is the most important thing (more important than understanding and learning, for instance), even if I'm doing better I'm still a failure because "I didn't get it right," and there is no need to think about the strategies I need and the process I used to arrive at my answer because "getting it right" is all that the teacher really cares about. Johnston (1997) indicates that if a student answers and the teacher's response is "Wrong," the student is likely to not voluntarily respond again. This, he says, will lead children to become passive in their reading and will deprive children of the opportunity to learn to self-correct their own responses (p. 29). Similarly, Kohn (1993) cautions that "students who are afraid of making mistakes are unlikely to ask for help when they need it, unlikely to feel safe enough to take intellectual risks, and unlikely to be intrinsically motivated" (p. 213).

Research has previously been cited concerning the importance of children's motivation and self-perceptions. Additional research suggests that focusing on "getting it right" *or giving students tasks with only one "right" or "acceptable" answer is not a good idea.* For instance, Turner (1995) found that first-grade children who were asked to focus on tasks with only one correct answer showed less motivation and less use of reading and learning strategies. Findings from the 1994 NAEP indicate also that older students who are more frequently given opportunities to discuss *various* interpretations of what they read and to explain their understanding show higher proficiency in reading than students who are given these opportunities less frequently (Campbell, Donahue, Reese, and Phillips 1996, 72). Finally, Johnston (1984) concludes that "instead of a concern over response outcomes, right or wrong, there needs to be greater concern over the reasons behind the responses" (p. 175).

Focusing on skills and using skill sheets excessively can lead to little time for focusing on comprehension and reading real books and literature. Needless to say, few reading educators, including "the experts" in this study, think this is a good idea. For instance, Allington (1997) reports that studies of exemplary teachers indicate that they teach phonics knowledge and strategies to children *rather than* assigning pages in phonics workbooks. Others have indicated that priorities are out of balance when young children are made to concentrate on letter, sound matching, letter discrimination, and letter names, and when teachers give only scant attention to activities that involve children with stories (Hiebert and McWhorter 1987; Teale and Sulzby 1989). Hiebert (1994) indicates that a regimen of skill and drill for students who depend on schools to become literate fails to help them become readers and writers who engage in literacy as a lifelong pursuit, and she cites research with second-language learners to prove her point (Commins and Miramontes 1989; Moll and Diaz 1987).

Using a basal without modification is likewise not recommended. In their well-known report, *Becoming a Nation of Readers*, Anderson, Hiebert, Scott, and Wilkinson (1985) suggest that there is ample evidence that independent reading does much more to develop reading ability than all the workbooks and practice sheets children typically must complete in a basal reading program (pp. 75–76). Therefore, it obviously follows that if a basal were to be used "slavishly" and without modification, children could be doing far more workbook and practice pages than necessary, taking time away from the more productive activity of really reading!

Although criticisms of basals abound (for instance, Baumann 1992; Goodman, Shannon, Freeman, and Murphy 1988; Shannon and Goodman 1994; and Weaver 1989), it seems overall that a good many of these criticisms could be negated by more careful and selective use of the basal materials and assignments, modifying them as needed, based on children's needs and interests and teachers' purposes.

The experts in my study, as well as many others who are knowledgeable about reading instruction and learning, do not think ability grouping is a good idea either. In fact, most reading educators and researchers believe that long-term ability grouping is detrimental to the reading development of many children (see for example Allington 1980, 1983, 1995; Barr 1989; Barr and Dreeben 1991; Hiebert 1983; Indrisano and Parratore 1991; Oakes 1992; Shannon 1985; Weinstein 1976). Ability grouping leads to the "low-group" designated children being treated differently from children in the "high groups"; they tend to be given more drill work rather than higher quality reading instruction, remain in the low group, develop negative self-concepts, and dislike reading. Children in the "middle group" tend to be treated as mediocre and often experience many of the same problems as children assigned to the low group. Conversely, high-group children are treated with more respect, are allowed to do more independent reading, and usually are given a higher quality of reading instruction or assignments; and, of course, they tend to like reading more (Flippo 1997a, 30–31). Even so, Slavin's research and analysis (1987, 1991) indicate that high-group children would do just as well if they were not ability-grouped or tracked at all. (For additional consequences of ability grouping, see Optiz 1998, 17.)

Requiring children to be tested after every skill taught and every story read can lead to children becoming bored and over-tested. Testing takes time. (For instance, Murphy, 1994, reviewed the 1989–1992 testing programs of major basal series and found that if first graders were required to complete all the tests for their respective programs, they would be tested on from 373 to 1,086 items.) This time could be better spent for real reading. Research reports have indicated that children get better at reading by reading, and time for reading is critical (Braunger and Lewis 1997, 54). There is little purpose to taking the time for testing after every skill taught, unless you believe that children cannot move on to "the next" skill before learning a prerequisite skill. Most reading researchers, as well as the experts in the study, no longer believe in sequencing skill development. (For example, see Adams 1990; Allington 1995; and Johnston 1984).

Johnston (1984) indicates that "hierarchical models of reading have found little support in the literature" and "reading does not consist of a set of discrete subskills" (p. 160). Dole, Duffy, Roehler, and Pearson (1991) agree that the hierarchical view, emphasizing sequential development and skill mastery, is no longer supported. Adams (1990) further asserts that "the process of reading cannot be divided into key and support activities. All of its component knowledge and skills must work together within a single integrated and interdependent system. And it is in that way that they must be acquired as well" (p. 423). Finally, Weaver (1989) indicates that teaching reading one skill at a time may in fact mitigate against students developing abilities to analyze, evaluate, and extend what they read, as well as to read well enough to solve everyday problems in adult life. To make her point, she cites the analyses by Applebee, Langer, and Mullis (1987) and Venezky, Kaestle, and Sum (1987, 28, 44–46) of several different NAEP assessments.

Taking the time for testing after every story read also doesn't make sense, unless you are sure that if students don't "know" story A, they could not read story B. If so, wouldn't a group discussion regarding the plot and events of story A and predictions from the students concerning what might happen next, in story B, suffice?

We also know, based on the previously cited research reports by Nagy and colleagues (1985), that since children learn most of their vocabulary from actually reading, it would not make sense to hold them back from the "next" story or book simply because they can't demonstrate on a test that they know all the words!

The experts believe in, and other research supports, the benefits of modeling and providing multiple demonstrations of how reading is done and used. This modeling includes the reading we do to show children that we enjoy reading and that reading is useful to us, too, as teachers. It also includes the instructional guidance and support we provide when we model, scaffold, and demonstrate how we read different types of text, how we figure out text, and the strategies we use as readers to get meaning from text. Modeling and scaffolding are widely accepted as a way for teachers to structure reading support for children and demonstrate the reading process (for instance, Applebee and Langer 1983; Braunger and Lewis 1997; Brown, Palincsar, and Armbuster 1994; Duffy, Roehler, and Herrmann 1988; Roehler and Duffy 1991).

Silent reading allows children to focus on the meaning of what they are reading, rather than focusing on their "performance" as often happens during oral readings. Therefore, the experts agree that silent reading should be used whenever appropriate during instructional and other reading times. Others also agree as to the importance of silent reading. Taylor, Frye, and Maruyama (1990) found, for instance, that the amount of silent reading done in school was a significant predictor of growth in reading comprehension. The study by Evans and Carr (1985) showed that, of various teacher-led activities, the silent reading of text had the highest correlation with reading comprehension. Wilkinson and Anderson's 1992 study indicated that silent reading allows children to read more words in a given time period, and other research has shown that the more students read, the better they become at reading. Also, Wilkinson and Anderson found that silent reading allowed students to become engaged with the text and focus their attention on gaining meaning. Smith and Elley's (1997) review of research studies shows also the benefits of silent reading.

This is not to say that students should never read orally. The experts in this study would support use of oral reading for assessment purposes (for instance, oral reading is necessary in order to do miscue analysis, running records, and informal reading inventories [IRI]). Additionally, the experts in this study would also support the use of oral reading for activities such as readers' theatre; selections of poetry, limericks, and rhymes; shared readings; orally rereading parts of a story that pertain to the discussion; and during individual conferences with children. Others agree. For example, see Braunger and Lewis (1997, 50) and Johnston (1997, 193).

Finally, although discussed elsewhere, the experts do agree that reading instruction should be planned so that students engage in purposeful reading and writing as part of the activity and their individual follow-up work. The research supports this. When children are reading and writing for real purposes they are much more likely to be engaged in the activity. It has already been explained that this engagement leads to higher reading achievement. Additionally, related research suggests that reading for real, genuine purposes relates strongly to the frequency with which children read, and that enjoyment of reading is a positive predictor of children's reading performance (Wigfield, Wilde, Baker, Fernandez-Fein, and Scher 1996). Hiebert (1994) recommends authentic literacy tasks in order to allow children to take ownership of their literacy and schooling (pp. 404–405). She explains authentic literacy tasks as ones in which reading and writing serve a function for children, and involve children in the immediate use of literacy (p. 391).

My Interpretation

I grouped the experts' agreements that seemed to say "something" about reading instruction under this category because I believe that politically it is important that we know what they (the experts) do agree on about reading instruction. However, I want to again remind readers of this book, at this juncture, that this study and book are *not* about how to teach reading. We have instead been just looking at agreements concerning contexts and practices for reading. The agreements in this category simply indicate which practices the experts believe would make learning to read difficult and which would facilitate it. The actual teaching methods, approaches, strategies, techniques, and activities are up to the teacher to be decided, planned, and carried out based on the teacher's consideration of the needs, strategies, and motivations of the child and the context of the situation and classroom.

Experts have not agreed to all the dimensions and aspects that one could possibly cluster under the heading "reading instruction." Clearly, many important areas are not listed. However, what they have agreed to could serve as a beginning regarding contexts and practices for classroom instruction. Using this beginning, I have developed two additional classroom portraits that I hope exemplify some of the agreements clustered in this category (particularly some that haven't appeared in the other portraits). I am hoping that teachers responding to this book will later share others from their own classroom practice.

Ms. Chang's First-Grade Class

Ms. Chang believes that it is important to teach phonics and other word recognition skills as well as to emphasize and teach strategies to develop comprehension. Therefore, she focuses equally on both important aspects of teaching reading in her classroom. She uses the language experience approach (LEA) to teach many of the phonics and word recognition skills, as well as to help children develop a sight vocabulary. She also believes that by using children's ideas, words, and syntax to write the LEA stories about things they are interested in or have read about, she is helping to make her reading and writing activities meaningful and purposeful.

Ms. Chang keeps a chart of all the sounds, blends, and digraphs she has taught within the context of the LEA stories she's written with the children. She also keeps a chart of all the sight words that she has emphasized, and these charts, along with the LEA stories, are proudly displayed in the classroom for children to refer to and read whenever they desire. She encourages children to demonstrate how well they can orally read these stories when she conferences with them individually. She also uses those opportunities to have them demonstrate their recognition of some of the sight words they have learned. Children illustrate the LEA stories focusing on what they were about (comprehension). Children share their pictures and display them under the LEA stories on the classroom walls. Sometimes children publish their LEA's by having Ms. Chang help them type their stories onto their own computer disks and print them. Ms. Chang lets them add to their stories, edit them, or change them anytime they wish.

Ms. Chang also reads many books and stories to the children. When she does this she models good reading and uses the opportunity to talk about the story and how she is able to figure out a difficult word (from the way it looks and sounds, and for its "fit" in the story, asking herself, does this fit and sound right [syntax] and does this make sense [semantics]?). She asks the children comprehension questions about the reading and when they answer, she asks them how they knew. She gives them a chance to explain how they knew. If the child's answer doesn't "quite" make sense, she asks probing questions and "scaffolds" to help shape the responses for a "better fit," complimenting the child on his good ideas or good work. She also models and demonstrates how she is able to figure out the answer. All of the children's participation is valued and if the children want her to read the story again and again, she always does.

Ms. Chang encourages the children to read many picture books and other easy books. She encourages silent reading whenever possible. Each day she asks children if they would like to share a book they have read. Each day she picks one or two different children to share. When children share, they hold up the book, show the pictures, and tell about it. Ms. Chang often reads the book aloud. The children who shared the book can ask comprehension questions about the book and Ms. Chang and the children try to answer. Whoever answers is asked to tell how he knew the answer (metacognition). Ms. Chang always models and demonstrates how she arrived at the answer too.

Mrs. Feinstein's Second-Grade Class

Mrs. Feinstein does not believe in ability grouping children, nor does she believe in teaching skills or words in isolation; but she does like the basal program her school has adopted, and she uses it as part of her instructional program. To avoid ability grouping, she organizes her reading instruction around children's skills and strategies. There are no high or low groups, just flexible groups that focus on particular skills and/or strategies; these groups can change. No one is frozen in any of the groups. For example, children who have shown the need to work on various word recognition skills meet with her at least once a day for this work. Children who do not need to work on the(se) particular skill(s) do not take part in this group; however, she will meet with other skill/strategy groups at other times. Some children are in several groups. After silently reading a selection from their basal, she and the children discuss the selection, first focusing on the story and meaning, and then she goes back to point out and reinforce the word recognition skills (phonics or other skills) that she and the children may have used to figure out new or difficult words. Work sheets and other materials focusing on the needed word recognition skills for the text of the story read, which are appropriate for the children's needs and are provided with the basal, are sometimes used as follow-up practice when she thinks individual children need it. If Mrs. Feinstein doesn't think particular worksheets or workbook pages are appropriate, or if she feels that they are too decontextualized, she will not use them. She is very selective about these practice materials. Sometimes she figures out better ways of practicing a needed skill and contextualizing the practice.

In addition to the basal selections and appropriate skill and strategy group follow-ups, Mrs. Feinstein also believes that many opportunities for writing and many opportunities for reading other books and literature are desirable for further developing her students' word recognition and other reading skills and strategies. Therefore, Mrs. Feinstein and all her students take part in sustained silent reading twice a day, and all children are given frequent opportunities to write about their readings, or about other things they are interested in. Mrs. Feinstein encourages all kinds of writing activity because she believes that writing and use of invented spelling will help children further develop their phonics and other word recognition skills.

She frequently observes children as they read, write, and work, and visits "around" to see how they are doing; she uses these observations along with her observations of their work in the skill and strategy groups for assessing children's literacy development. Additionally, samples of children's writing are kept in a folder for each child. Notations about their word recognition and comprehension skills are also added each month when she uses a running record to individually assess each child's oral reading strategies and uses retellings to assess their comprehension (following the running records).

In Closing: A Reflection

Readers should note that throughout the process of seeking agreements, the experts, regardless of their perspective, always refrained from endorsing or suggesting any one particular method or approach to teaching reading. Clearly they know, as major respected studies have suggested, there is no one method or approach that is best for all children in all situations. For example, the famous and often cited first-grade studies, compiled by Bond and Dykstra (1967), indicated that no one instructional method was superior to others for students at either high or low levels of reading readiness. These studies involved twenty-seven research projects all over the United States to test out various instructional approaches. *What made the difference in reading success was the teachers and the learning situations they created!*

In more recent years, others have agreed that there can be no such thing as one universal method (Adams 1990, 423), and because of the overriding influence of contextual conditions, a strategy may prove effective in one situation but not in another (Barr in press). Instead, what seems very important is that teachers are knowledgeable (Snow et al. 1998); aware of the key choices they make in establishing, guiding, and altering their literacy programs (Barr in press); and that children have access to meaningful print (McQuillan 1998).

We all know there are no simple solutions or panaceas, and they will not be forthcoming (Pearson 1996). Reading is a complex process (see, for instance, the IRA 1997 and NCTE 1997 statements). But based on their many years of research and practice, the experts collectively do agree on the contexts and practices which have been specified by this study. Even though these agreements clearly do not include every aspect or area related to reading development, they are still agreements about contexts and practices for classroom reading (which you will have an opportunity to respond to later). Additionally, these agreements do not point to any particular method or approach. Teachers who use a variety of methods and approaches should be able to consider the contexts and practices suggested by the experts in this study.

In the chapters that follow, expert teachers will consider and reflect on these findings. Then it is your turn!

References

Adams, M. 1990. *Beginning to Read: Thinking and Learning About Print.* Cambridge, MA: MIT Press.

Allington, R. L. 1980. "Poor Readers Don't Get to Read Much in Reading Groups." *Language Arts* 57 (8): 873–875.

———. 1983. "The Reading Instruction Provided Readers of Different Reading Abilities." *The Elementary School Journal* 83 (5): 548–559.

———. 1995. "Literacy Lessons in the Elementary Schools: Yesterday, Today, and Tomorrow." In *No Quick Fix: Rethinking Literacy Programs in America's Elementary Schools*, ed. R.L. Allington and S.A. Walmsley, 1–15. New York: Teachers College Press. Newark, DE: International Reading Association.

———. August/September 1997. "Overselling Phonics: Five Unscientific Assertions About Reading Instruction." *Reading Today* 15 (1): 15–16.

Anderson, R.C., E.H. Hiebert, J.A. Scott, and I.A.G. Wilkinson. 1985. *Becoming a Nation of Readers*. Champaign, IL: Center for the Study of Reading, National Institute of Education, and National Academy of Education.

Applebee, A. and J. Langer. 1983. "Instructional Scaffolding: Reading and Writing as Natural Activities." *Language Arts* 60 (2): 168–175.

Applebee, A.N., J.A. Langer, and I.V.S. Mullis. 1987. *Learning to Be Literate in America: Reading, Writing, and Reasoning*. Princeton, NJ: National Assessment of Educational Progress, Educational Testing Service.

Barr, R. 1989. "The Social Organization of Literacy Instruction." In *Cognitive and Social Perspectives for Literacy Research and Instruction*, ed. S. McCormick and J. Zutell, 19–33. The Thirty-Eighth Yearbook of the National Reading Conference. Chicago: National Reading Conference.

———. In press. "Research on the Teaching of Reading." In *Handbook of Research on Teaching*, 4th ed., ed. V. Richardson. Washington, DC: American Educational Research Association.

Barr, R. and R. Dreeben. 1991. "Grouping Students for Reading Instruction." In *Handbook of Reading Research*, vol. 2, ed. R. Barr, M.L. Kamil, P. Mosenthal, and P.D. Pearson, 885–910. New York: Longman.

Baumann, J.F. 1992. "Basal Reading Programs and the Deskilling of Teachers: A Critical Examination of the Argument." *Reading Research Quarterly* 27 (4): 390–398.

Baumann, J.F. and A.M. Duffy. 1997. *Engaged Reading for Pleasure and Learning: A Report from the National Reading Research Center*. Athens, GA: National Reading Research Center.

Bond, G.L. and R. Dykstra. 1967. "The Cooperative Research Program in First-Grade Reading Instruction." *Reading Research Quarterly* 2 (4): 5–142.

Braunger, J. and J.P. Lewis. 1997. *Building a Knowledge Base in Reading*. Portland, OR: Northwest Regional Laboratory. Urbana, IL: National Council of Teachers of English. Newark, DE: International Reading Association.

Brown, A.L., A.S. Palincsar, and B.B. Armbruster. 1994. "Instructing Comprehension-Fostering Activities in Interactive Learning Situations." In *Theoretical Models and Processes of Reading*, 4th ed., ed. R.B. Ruddell, M.R. Ruddell, and H. Singer, 757–787. Newark, DE: International Reading Association.

Campbell, J.R., P.L. Donahue, C.M. Reese, and G.W. Phillips. 1996. *NAEP 1994 Reading Report Card for the Nation and the States: Findings from the National Assessment of Educational Progress and Trial State Assessment.* Princeton, NJ: National Center for Education Statistics, Educational Testing Service.

Commins, N.L. and O.B. Miramontes. 1989. "Perceived and Actual Linguistic Competence: A Descriptive Study of Four Low-Achieving Hispanic Bilingual Students." *American Educational Research Journal* 26 (4): 443–472.

Cunningham, A.E. 1990. "Explicit Versus Implicit Instruction in Phonemic Awareness." *Journal of Experimental Child Psychology* 50 (3): 429–444.

Delpit, L. 1988. "The Silenced Dialogue: Power and Pedagogy in Educating Other People's Children." *Harvard Educational Review* 58 (3): 280–298.

Dole, J.A., G.G. Duffy, L.R. Roehler, and P.D. Pearson. 1991. "Moving from the Old to the New: Research on Reading Comprehension Instruction." *Review of Educational Research* 61 (2): 239–264.

Duffy, G.G., L.R. Roehler, and B.A. Herrmann. 1988. "Modeling Mental Processes Helps Poor Readers Become Strategic Readers." *The Reading Teacher* 41 (8): 762–767.

Evans, M. and T. Carr. 1985. "Cognitive Abilities, Conditions of Learning, and the Early Development of Reading Skill." *Reading Research Quarterly* 20 (3): 327–350.

Flippo, R.F. 1997a. *Reading Assessment and Instruction: A Qualitative Approach to Diagnosis.* Ft. Worth, TX: Harcourt Brace College Publishers.

———. 1997b. "Sensationalism, Politics, and Literacy: What's Going On?" *Phi Delta Kappan* 79(4): 301–304.

Gambrell, L., B. Palmer, and R. Codling. 1993. *Motivation to Read.* Washington, DC: U.S. Department of Education, Office of Educational Research and Improvement.

Gambrell, L.B., B.M. Palmer, R.M. Codling, and S.A. Mazzoni. 1996. "Assessing Motivation to Read." *The Reading Teacher* 49 (7): 518–533.

Goodman, K.S., P. Shannon, Y.S. Freeman, and S. Murphy. 1988. *Report Card on Basal Readers.* Katonah, NY: Richard C. Owen Publishers.

Guthrie, J.T. 1996. "Educational Contexts for Engagement in Literacy." *The Reading Teacher* 49 (6): 432–445.

———. January 1997. "The Director's Corner." *NRRC News: A Newsletter of the National Reading Research Center*, 3.

Hiebert, E.H. 1983. "An Examination of Ability Grouping for Reading Instruction." *Reading Research Quarterly* 18 (2): 231–255.

———. 1994. "Becoming Literate Through Authentic Tasks: Evidence and Adaptations." In *Theoretical Models and Processes of Reading*, 4th ed., ed. R.B. Ruddell, M.R. Ruddell, and H. Singer, 391–413. Newark, DE: International Reading Association.

Hiebert, E.H. and L. McWhorter. 1987. *The Content of Kindergarten and Readiness Books in Four Basal Reading Programs.* Paper presented at the annual meeting of the American Educational Research Association. Washington, DC.

Hoffman, J. 1981. "Is There a Legitimate Place for Oral Reading Instruction in a Developmental Reading Program?" *Elementary School Journal* 81 (5): 305–310.

Indrisano, R. and J. Parratore. 1991. "Classroom Contexts for Literacy Learning." In *Handbook of Research on Teaching the English Language Arts*, ed. J. Flood, J. Jensen, D. Lapp, and J. Squire, 477–488. New York: Macmillan.

International Reading Association. January 1997. "The Role of Phonics in Reading Instruction: A Position Statement of the International Reading Association." Newark, DE: International Reading Association.

Johnston, P.H. 1984. "Assessment in Reading." In *Handbook of Reading Research*, ed. P.D. Pearson and section ed. R. Barr, M.L. Kamil, and P. Mosenthal, 147–182. New York: Longman.

————. 1997. *Knowing Literacy: Constructive Literacy Assessment.* York, ME: Stenhouse.

Kohn, A. 1993. *Punished by Rewards: The Trouble with Gold Stars, Incentive Plans, A's, Praise, and Other Bribes.* New York: Houghton Mifflin.

McQuillan, J. 1998. *The Literacy Crisis: False Claims, Real Solutions.* Portsmouth, NH: Heinemann.

Moll, L.C. and S. Diaz. 1987. "Change as the Goal of Educational Research." *Anthropology and Education Quarterly* 18 (4): 300–311.

Morrow, L.M. 1996. *Motivating Reading and Writing in Diverse Classrooms: Social and Physical Contexts in a Literature-based Program.* Research Report No. 28. Urbana, IL: National Council of Teachers of English.

Moustafa, M. 1997. *Beyond Traditional Phonics: Research Discoveries and Reading Instruction.* Portsmouth, NH: Heinemann.

Murphy, S. 1994. "Neither Gone Nor Forgotten: Testing in New Basal Readers." In *Basal Readers: A Second Look*, ed. P. Shannon and K. Goodman, 103–113. Katonah, NY: Richard C. Owen Publishers.

Nagy, W.E. and P.A. Herman. 1985. "Incidental vs. Instructional Approaches to Increasing Reading Vocabulary." *Educational Perspectives* 23 (1): 16–21.

Nagy, W.E., P.A. Herman, and R.C. Anderson. 1985. "Learning Words from Context." *Reading Research Quarterly* 20 (2): 233–253.

National Council of Teachers of English. November 1997. "On Phonics as a Part of Reading Instruction." Urbana, IL: National Council of Teachers of English.

Nicholson, T. 1991. "Do Children Read Words Better in Context or in Lists?" A Classic Study Revisited. *Journal of Educational Psychology* 83 (4): 444–450.

Oakes, J. 1992. "Can Tracking Research Inform Practice?" *Educational Researcher* 21 (4): 12–21.

Optiz, M.F. 1998. *Flexible Grouping in Reading: Practical Ways to Help All Students Become Better Readers.* New York: Scholastic Professional Books.

Pearson, P.D. 1996. "Six Ideas in Search of a Champion: What Policymakers Should

Know About the Teaching and Learning of Literacy in Our Schools." *Journal of Literacy Research* 28 (2): 302–309.

Pressley, M., J. Rankin, and L. Yokoi. 1996. "A Survey of the Instructional Practices of Primary Teachers Nominated as Effective in Promoting Literacy." *The Elementary School Journal* 96 (4): 363–384.

Purcell-Gates, V., E. McIntyre, and P. Freppon. 1995. "Learning Written Storybook Language in School: A Comparison of Low-SES Children in Skills-Based and Whole Language Classrooms." *American Educational Research Journal* 32 (3): 659–685.

Roehler, L.R. and G.G. Duffy. 1991. "Teachers' Instructional Actions." In *Handbook of Reading Research*, vol. 2, ed. R. Barr, M.L. Kamil, P. Mosenthal, and P.D. Pearson, 861–883. New York: Longman.

Samuels, S.J. 1988. "Decoding and Automaticity: Helping Poor Readers Become Automatic at Word Recognition." *The Reading Teacher* 41 (8): 756–760.

Shannon, P. 1985. "Reading Instruction and Social Class." *Language Arts* 62 (6): 604–613.

Shannon, P. and K. Goodman, ed. 1994. *Basal Readers: A Second Look.* Katonah, NY: Richard C. Owen Publishers.

Simmons, H. and P. Ammon. 1989. "Child Knowledge and Primerese Text: Mismatches and Miscues." *Research in the Teaching of English* 23 (4): 380–398.

Slavin, R.E. 1987. "Ability Grouping and Student Achievement in Elementary Schools: A Best-Evidence Synthesis." *Review of Educational Research* 57 (3): 293–336.

———. 1991. "Are Cooperative Learning and 'Untracking' Harmful to the Gifted?" *Educational Leadership* 48 (6): 68–71.

Smith, J. and W. Elley. 1997. *How Children Learn to Read.* Katonah, NY: Richard C. Owen Publishers.

Snow, C.E., M.S. Burns, and P. Griffin. ed. 1998. *Preventing Reading Difficulties in Young Children.* Washington, DC: National Research Council, National Academy Press.

Taubenheim, B. and J. Christensen. 1978. "Let's Shoot 'Cock Robin'! Alternatives to Round Robin Reading." *Language Arts* 55 (8): 975–977.

Taylor, D., B. Frye, and G. Maruyama. 1990. "Time Spent Reading and Reading Growth." *American Educational Research Journal* 27 (2): 351–362.

Taylor, N. and U. Connor. 1982. "Silent vs. Oral Reading: The Rational Instructional Use of Both Processes." *The Reading Teacher* 35 (4): 440–443.

Teale, W.H. and E. Sulzby. 1989. "Emergent Literacy: New Perspectives." In *Emerging Literacy: Young Children Learn to Read and Write*, ed. D.S. Strickland and L.M. Morrow, 1–15. Newark, DE: International Reading Association.

Tierney, R.J. and T. Shanahan. 1991. "Research on the Reading-Writing Relationship: Interactions, Transactions, and Outcomes." In *Handbook of Reading Research*, vol. 2, ed. R. Barr, M.L. Kamil, P. Mosenthal, and P.D. Pearson, 246–280. New York: Longman.

Tobias, S. 1994. "Interest, Prior Knowledge, and Learning." *Review of Educational Research* 64 (1): 37–54.

Turner, J.C. 1995. "The Influence of Classroom Contexts on Young Children's Motivation for Literacy." *Reading Research Quarterly* 30 (3): 410–441.

Venezky, R.L., C.F. Kaestle, and A.M. Sum. 1987. *The Subtle Danger: Reflections on the Literacy Abilities of America's Young Adults.* Princeton, NJ: Center for the Assessment of Educational Progress, Educational Testing Service.

Weaver, C. 1989. "The Basalization of America: A Cause for Concern." In *Two Reactions to the Report Card on Basal Readers*, ed. C.B. Smith, 4–7, 14–22 and 31–37. Bloomington, IN: ERIC Clearinghouse on Reading and Communication Skills.

Weinstein, R.S. 1976. "Reading Group Membership in First Grade: Teacher Behaviors and Pupil Experience Over Time." *Journal of Education Psychology* 68 (1): 103–116.

Wigfield, A., K. Wilde, L. Baker, S. Fernandez-Fein, and D. Scher. 1996. *The Nature of Children's Motivations for Reading, and Their Relations to Reading Frequency and Reading Performance.* Athens, GA: National Reading Research Center.

Wilkinson, I. and R. Anderson. 1992. *Micro-Experimental Analysis of the Small-Group Reading Lesson: Social and Cognitive Consequences of Silent Reading.* Champaign, IL: Center for the Study of Reading.

5

I Had No Choice!
Learning from the Experts

GAY FAWCETT

Most new teachers (and even some veterans) are so consumed with the day-to-day concerns of schedules, discipline, lesson plans, and grading papers that they do not take the time to study what experts in the field are saying about teaching and learning. Well, I was different. Early in my first year of teaching I began studying what the experts had to say about literacy learning. I can't really claim it as some badge of honor, though. I simply had no choice!

I was the first in my family to attend college. My blue-collar family did not know how to choose a "good" college. We didn't even know there was such a thing. We did know, however, that some were cheaper than others, and so I headed off to a state university near home that my steel-mill father could afford. I realize now that I did not have the best of educations, but it was good enough to land me a teaching job in a factory town similar to the one I grew up in.

I had taken only one methods course in the teaching of reading. To make matters worse, I took it in a five-week summer program, and it was taught by a local building principal who was certainly not a literacy expert! When the course was over, I promptly sold the textbook back to the university used bookstore where it had been purchased. When faced with the daunting task of teaching twenty-eight first graders to read, the only thing I could remember about the course was that *digraph* only has one *a*. (One of the principal's pet peeves was when the word was misspelled as *diagraph*.) It did not take me long to recognize my inadequacy. I did not know how to teach these children to read. I would have to learn from the experts. I had no choice!

My Experts

Expert Adrian Bell

Adrian was my first expert. Esther, the school psychologist, had tested Adrian during his kindergarten year and told me during the new teacher orientation that Adrian could already read. I didn't really believe it until weeks later when Adrian came to his first day of school and proceeded straight to the bulletin board to read every classmate's name. His only mistake was that he pronounced Sean's name phonetically (Seen), following the rule I didn't learn in college— something about "when two vowels go walking." I was baffled by Adrian. I didn't know some children could read before a teacher taught them. For a few weeks I ignored Adrian's reading. I had no way to even think about it.

Adrian was a happy and social child. Because he could already read, I saw no need to worry about which reading group he was in, so I let him choose. Some days he would come to the reading table with his best friend (Adrian still called him Seen rather than Sean) even though that group was struggling just to learn the alphabet. Other days Adrian would come with the top group who was reading pretty well, albeit not as well as Adrian. I saw no need to do anything extra for Adrian because I had my hands full trying to figure out how to teach the other twenty-seven children.

Adrian was actually a big help to me because he could read. When I was working with reading groups, Adrian would help other children who were working at their seats if they got stuck on words. Because he could read everyone's name, Adrian took the lunch count and attendance each day while I busied myself giving extra attention to students who were falling behind. Sometimes Adrian wrote playground plans with assigned roles and tasks for his friends. Of course Adrian made lots of spelling errors and he wasn't un-limited in his reading ability, but Adrian was way ahead of the other first graders so I continued to ignore my obligation to do something more for Adrian.

Then, suddenly, I had no choice. Esther approached me in the hall one day to talk about Adrian. Esther was a very large woman who stood twelve inches from your face when she talked. Behind her back the teachers called her "Esther the Tester," but no one crossed Esther! She demanded to know what I was doing for Adrian. I made it up on the spot: "I've decided to put him in the second grade reader." "Good," she replied, "I'll be in to check on him in a few weeks." A few days later Adrian was in a reading group all by himself, reading aloud from the second grade reader. And the happy, social child that I had ignored suddenly became a passive, quiet child that worried me.

In college I hadn't learned how to help children like Adrian. I was so new to the profession that I didn't even know about journals like *The Reading Teacher* and *Language Arts*, and, although they were giants in the field, I had never heard of Ed Fry, Yetta Goodman, or Rand Spiro. I would have to learn from Adrian. He would be my expert. I had no choice!

I had no idea how Adrian had learned to read and write, but I did know that literacy was a natural part of how he got things done, so I began watching how Adrian used reading and writing. I always posted the lunch menu on the classroom door so that I could be prepared for the daily question, "What's for lunch today?" Adrian would read it before going home in the afternoon so that he could decide whether to pack or buy the next day. One day he wrote a letter to a child who had recently moved away and asked if I would mail it. His mother told me he helped in the grocery store by reading the labels and picking up food items from one side of the aisle while she did the other side.

What I learned from Adrian, my expert, was what the experts cited in this book articulate so well. Adrian was happiest with reading and writing, not when he sat at the reading table with a second grade book, but when the literacy task was functional for him. Adrian knew intuitively what our experts agree on: Adrian was convinced that reading did further the purpose of his life. My six-year-old expert knew, as do the professional experts, the importance of purposeful reading and writing.

I decided that I would let Adrian make his way independently through the second grade reader. That would keep Esther happy, and Adrian could continue to choose functional literacy activities with the time he would have spent reading aloud in his own lonely group. Although I was not consciously aware of this practice, what I did was provide the context and environment that would facilitate learning to read. Most of the time Adrian provided his own purpose, but I also began looking for new ways to have him help me with tasks that involved reading and writing. Adrian knew a lot about literacy—Adrian was my expert.

Expert Beth Moore

I made up for all the worrying I did not invest in Adrian by worrying twice as much about Beth. Beth's mother requested a parent/teacher conference the week before school started. Mrs. Moore said I needed to know something disturbing about Beth before the first day of school. I listened with dread, expecting to hear about some sort of custody battle or health problem (Fawcett 1994).

"Beth has dyslexia," she said. This was not at all what I had been expecting. How could Mrs. Moore say that her little girl had dyslexia when Beth had not even had first grade instruction? "How do you know?" I asked. "Her kindergarten teacher said so. She couldn't learn the Letter People and Miss Kathy wanted us to keep her in kindergarten, but my husband was really upset about that. He's a teacher, you know." I was alarmed about Beth. Was she really dyslexic? Should I request that Esther test her? How would I teach her? And what is dyslexia anyway?

Beth was a tiny 5-year-old when she started first grade. She was an attractive child with large blue eyes and blond curls, but she always looked tired because of the dark circles under her eyes. She rarely smiled, and had already begun to develop a failure complex. Her most frequent words were, "I can't."

I asked Esther for help, but her caseload was so heavy that she wanted to delay testing Beth. She did, however, bring a reading kit to my class and told me that if I used it Beth might read. I decided to form a small reading group made up of Beth and two other struggling readers—also dyslexic?, I wondered. I was not comfortable with the kit. I found the materials boring, and despite my lack of knowledge and experience, I still somehow felt insulted by the scripted teacher's guide. The students were asked to make letter/sound associations as I flashed cards. There were no stories in the kit; those would come after the students learned the skills needed for "real" reading.

The students tried hard, but each day it was as if we were starting over. There was little retention of previous work. I was discouraged, but Mrs. Moore and Esther were pleased that I was attempting to adjust my instruction to Beth's needs.

Beth loved the picture books she checked out of the library. Often I would see her sitting in the reading corner of our classroom pretending to read to our stuffed Clifford. I concluded that Beth knew what reading was all about but that she would probably never be a reader because she was dyslexic.

One morning Beth came to my desk with a copy of Bill Martin's (1967) *Brown Bear, Brown Bear, What Do You See?* I am appalled now to think that I was a first-grade teacher and I did not know this book. Beth said, "Mrs. Fawcett, listen to this," and she read the entire book to me. She laughed out loud when she was done. I had never heard Beth laugh. I laughed too as I hugged her. She must have read the book to Clifford 50 times that week. I invited her to bring Clifford with her to the reading lessons, but she never did.

On Friday when the class visited the library to check out new books, Beth asked the librarian if she could keep the book another week. The librarian curtly said no. Beth refused to check out any books that day. I went to the library the next morning and signed the book out on a six-week teacher loan. When I showed it to her, Beth took the book and went straight to Clifford. I asked her if she would read it to her parents. She agreed, and I invited them to stop by after school one day.

I was discouraged with their response to Beth's reading of *Brown Bear*. They said that she had memorized the book and that this was not "real" reading. I felt that it was very real for Beth although I could not articulate why. I knew that she was onto something that I needed to know. I did not have access to writings by George Spache, Wayne Otto, or Scott Paris. I would have to trust Beth—I had no choice!

I took *Brown Bear* to Beth's reading group the next day. After hearing Beth read it one time, the other students chimed in on the second reading. Beth smiled. When Aaron said, "Hey! *Beth* starts like *Brown Bear!*" I knew it was "real" reading. I went to the library looking for more Bill Martin books and to my delight found an entire set of little books like *Brown Bear*. We put the reading kit away and began reading the little books. This was more "real" than the stilted lessons I had been teaching. I found similar materials to carry us through the year, and Beth smiled more and more.

Beth had led me to an important practice that would facilitate learning to read: develop positive self-perception and expectations. By putting away the reading kit, I was able to give my students lots of time and opportunity to read real books. Although some people considered Beth a slow learner, Beth was really an expert. She knew what she needed in order to read, and I learned from her—I had no choice!

Professional Experts

I wish I could claim that I always listened to my experts and made the right choices, but that just would not be true. There were times when my own school experiences boomed out over the children's voices. There were other times when I doubted my ability to make sense of it all and felt compelled to listen to the "experts" who created the workbooks and teacher's manuals I was given. There were still other times when I was intimidated by the likes of Esther, and then gave in to what my little experts said would make learning to read difficult. However, as I learned more about the profession—who and what to read, what workshops to attend, what conferences to go to—I began to hear professional expert voices that said the same things my little experts were saying.

Expert Jerry Harste

Thank goodness for the expert voice of Jerry Harste! For a few years, writing for my class was simply a matter of teaching how to correctly form letters. We had a handwriting workbook, and I could remember learning to print in my grade school years. Although Chicory was writing simple stories on her own time, Jeremy was writing notes to his friends, and Michelle was labeling pictures that she drew, I did not see the relationship to the reading and writing instruction taking place in my classroom.

Then a friend told me about Harste's work, and I ordered the book, *Language Stories & Literacy Lessons* (Harste, Woodward, and Burke 1984). My young experts were validated by these professional experts: Children know a great deal about written language before ever entering school; children learn language through using language in their attempts to communicate with others; language learning is understandable only when viewed within its social context. I began seeking ways to facilitate learning to read by combining reading with other language processes and by considering the contexts, environment, and purposes for reading.

I encouraged children to post notes to their friends on a bulletin board set aside for that purpose. I asked Chicory to retell the stories that she wrote, and other children began writing stories and asking to tell them to the class. I recognized the power of listening and began reading aloud to the class several times throughout the day. In addition, I recognized that the quiet classroom I remembered as a child would probably make learning to read difficult since children need to talk about and share the different kinds of reading they do.

Expert Jane Hansen

Excited by the response of my students to such practice, I began to search out other professional literature. I found Jane Hansen's (1987) book, *When Writers Read*, at an exhibit table at a conference, and Hansen convinced me of the reciprocal nature of reading and writing. Hansen maintained that the best writers in the classroom are those students who read the most.

At the time I was giving my students several phonics worksheets a day, but Hansen convinced me that by manipulating language in personally meaningful pieces, students are better prepared to decode text by applying graphophonic, semantic, and syntactic strategies they have used for encoding messages. I decided to try it, and replaced a few of the seatwork papers I gave my students with time to read and time to write.

My classroom library was nearly nonexistent, but I had kept the books and magazines my own two sons had outgrown, and I encouraged the children to contribute reading material from home. They brought in the expected (books they were tired of and old *Sesame Street* magazines), but we also got the unexpected (old issues of *Ladies Home Journal* and books that their older brothers and sisters no longer wanted). The children were provided with a variety of printed materials and literature, a practice that the professional experts agree would facilitate learning to read.

At the time, I had not studied the theory behind invented spelling (Read 1975), but I did notice that the children were becoming better spellers even on words that were not on the weekly spelling list. Reading had become a tool for learning to spell, and most of the time the children were engaged in purposeful reading and writing.

Expert P. David Pearson

"More comprehension instruction research was conducted between 1980 and 1990 than in all of the previous history of reading research" (Pearson 1993, 506). It came just at the time I was learning from the experts—the professionals and my own—about literacy instruction. Pearson helped me to understand the difference between checking for comprehension and teaching comprehension (Durkin 1978–1979).

Pearson claimed, and my little experts confirmed, that explicit instruction in comprehension strategies resulted in increases in students' ability to make sense of what they were reading. I demonstrated how I would solve a reading problem through thinking aloud my own processes. I guided them through comprehension strategies such as K-W-L (Ogle 1986), DRTA (Stauffer 1969), and ReQuest (Vacca and Vacca 1993), and gradually gave them more and more responsibility for performing the strategies on their own. I found, as Pearson claimed (1994), that this instruction was especially effective for students who could read words but did not remember what they had read.

One day my students were on the vocabulary section of the district required reading test. It was a typical testing atmosphere; the students were working quietly and intently. Suddenly, Dusty jumped out of his seat, ripped up his test, and threw it on the floor. He screamed at me through tears, "This is stupid! I can't do this! Why do you make us do this? You tell us to use context clues, and there's no context here." I sat wondering what to say to a seven-year-old who knew more about how he learned to read than the adults who wrote the test. Dusty, my expert, was telling me that the reading instruction that provided multiple repeated demonstrations of how reading is done had worked.

Expert Yetta Goodman

When I first began teaching, I noticed that the children sometimes substituted one word for another when reading. Even when the substitutions made sense (i.e., house for home or kitten for cat), I felt compelled to correct the children. Paul was an expert who taught me the fallacy of that practice.

Each time we returned from our weekly trip to the school library, I allowed the children time at their seats to enjoy the books they had checked out. One day I was sitting near Paul as he read his library book aloud. Paul was an average reader. He had chosen a book that was not too difficult, and he appeared to be reading fairly fluently. I scooted over to his desk and looked over his shoulder as he read. What I saw surprised me. The story was about a farmer and his children. Each time Paul came to the word *farmer*, he said *father*. That certainly made sense since the farmer was obviously a father. When Paul came to the word *mother*, he said *mom*. He got the names of the children right (Bob and Nan) except for Arthur, whom he called *Andrew*. This made sense since Arthur is not a common name these days, and we had a child named Andrew in our class. He made some errors that did not make sense, but each time he struggled to make meaning by rereading or looking to me for help. It was obvious from this that he was understanding the story, and he seemed so proud of his accomplishment that I decided it might not be so important to correct children's mistakes if they made sense. Once again I listened to my experts because I had no choice—I didn't know where to turn in order to find out what I should do.

Years later I realized that the little experts had been right again when I read Ken and Yetta Goodman's work on miscue analysis (Goodman, Watson, and Burke 1987). I learned to observe when children's miscues show a graphic and phonic relationship. I learned to watch for the processing of syntactic information. I learned from the professional experts that students use psycho-sociolinguistic strategies as they read. Most importantly, I learned that "To err is human" (Goodman and Goodman 1994, 104).

By respecting the students' miscues, I was creating a context that would facilitate learning to read. The children were developing positive self-perceptions and expectations about their ability to succeed. The Goodmans had confirmed what my expert, Paul, had demonstrated.

Expert Scott Paris

One type of miscue that I intuitively knew to ignore was the mispronouncing of a name. I had watched children struggle to sound out a difficult name to the point of losing comprehension of what they had been reading. So I often told children not to worry about a name—what was important was that they understood the story. "Call him Joe or Betty and go on," I encouraged them. I didn't know until years later that I was teaching the students to be strategic readers.

The building principal invited groups of children to her office from time to time to read aloud to her. One day a group from my class was invited, and they chose a story with Japanese characters to read to Ms. Schofield. They practiced before going to the office, and they did well except for struggling with the name *Nara Shimotaro*. I reminded them not to worry too much about the name, and they skipped happily to the office, books in hand. Later Ms. Schofield told me the following story.

The children were reading well, round robin fashion, when Marneka got stuck on the name. She paused, and Nicole leaned over and whispered, "Joe." Marneka continued without missing another beat, and the other children followed suit as they came upon the character's name. When the story was complete, Ms. Schofield asked the children why they had changed Naro Shimotaro's name to *Joe*. Nicole responded, "We knew it wasn't important if you knew his name. It was just important if you understood the story."

A few days later, however, I recognized the importance of what Paris et al. (Paris, Lipson, and Wixson 1994) so clearly advocate: "Children need to learn the conditions under which strategies are applied and not applied. Then they will know when and why to use them" (p. 805). I was reading aloud the folk tale of Tikki Tikki Tembo No So Rembo Cherry Berry Ruchi Pip Berry Pimbo. As you will recall, the boy fell into a well, but when the town folks told one another what happened, it took so long for them to say his name that they didn't get to the well in time, and the poor boy drowned. Suddenly it occurred to me what would have happened if a child were reading the story and decided to skip the name. We talked about when it would and would not be appropriate to skip a name. We decided that usually it would be fine, but sometimes names of people are important, especially in true stories. After that they looked for examples to illustrate when to skip and not to skip names. The students were becoming consciously strategic.

I began watching for other strategies that would facilitate learning to read, and over time I talked with the students about things like skimming, deciding if a word they didn't know the meaning of was necessary to understand the story, and how to use picture clues to help understand the story.

What I later learned from the work of Scott Paris (Paris and Miles 1981) and others was that one of the benefits of becoming a strategic reader is that students can analyze and talk about their own behavior. My students were not naturally experts on strategic reading. They seemed to need explicit instruction, but once they understood the process, they became experts and confirmed what the professional experts taught me. By providing multiple, repeated demonstrations of how reading is done or used, I was able to implement a practice that would facilitate learning to read.

Expert Richard Anderson

Anyone who has ever taught kindergarten or first grade knows that these young children are an exaggerated example of the importance of schema. Nearly every conversation with a child this age can result in long, detailed and personal stories related to the topic. Let someone mention during Show and Tell that their dog died, and you will have hours worth of stories from class members about their own pets, their relatives' pets, their neighbor's pets, some TV character's pets, and on and on. As a new teacher, I would sometimes get impatient with what I called *rambling* and would cut it off.

Learning about schema theory from Richard Anderson (1994) and others helped to convince me that "a reader's *schema*, or organized knowledge of the world, provides much of the basis for comprehending, learning, and remembering the ideas in stories and texts" (Anderson 1994, 469). Once I knew this, I invited children to talk about their personal experiences, and I worked hard to direct the *ramblings* toward the text we would be reading.

Around this time I also studied Garner's (1994) ideas about metacognition and developed a belief that it was important to teach learners to monitor their cognitive processes while reading. I began talking to the children about the importance of thinking about what they already knew and how it fit with what was in the text.

After a few years of teaching, I was asked to work with a student teacher who happened to be the daughter of a local university president (Fawcett 1990). She decided to teach a unit on careers, and in the course of the unit, she invited people from various careers to visit. Of course, the university president was invited to discuss his job. There was a question and answer period when the children asked how many hours a day he worked, what kind of office he had, and (to my embarrassment) how much money he made. Then Anna raised her hand with a question, and I still wonder where it came from. "Do you know what reading is?" she asked. This highly articulate and educated man looked at me, then back at the children; he was stumped. "Let me tell you," Anna replied. "It's when you put what you know with what the author said, and then it makes sense." My expert, Anna, knew what the professional experts had been studying for at least a decade: "A reader comprehends a message when he is able to bring to mind a schema that gives a good account of the objects and events described in the message" (Anderson 1994, 469).

What I learned from the *ramblings* of first graders, to the scholarly work of Anderson and Garner, to Anna's insightful statement helped me to provide reading instruction that would facilitate learning to read. The children and I were able to provide for one another multiple, repeated demonstrations of how reading is done or used.

Expert Brian Cambourne

In the mid-1980s I attended a workshop that seemed to tie it all together for me. In this workshop we studied the following practices that Cambourne claimed would facilitate learning to read. Cambourne (Brown and Cambourne 1987) called them "Conditions of Learning":

- *Immersion* in text of all kinds
- *Demonstrations* of how texts are constructed and used
- *Expectations* as a powerful influence on learners
- *Responsibility* of learners to make their own learning decisions
- *Use* of literacy in functional, nonartificial ways
- *Approximations* as essential for learning to occur
- *Response* from more knowledgeable others

This short but powerful list provided me an overview of practices that would facilitate learning to read. I laminated it and taped it to the top of my desk. I still had much to learn from other experts—both the professionals and my students—but this list kept some of the most important concepts in front of me all the time.

Conclusion

In those early days of listening to my experts, I was young and inexperienced and I didn't always understand what I was learning. I didn't even know about the "Great Debate" (Chall 1967), much less have developed a stance! All I knew was that I had twenty-eight first graders that needed to learn to read, and I had no choice—they were the only experts I had. As it turned out, they were pretty good experts! What I learned from them was confirmed by the professional experts whose work I studied as time went on.

What I now know is that those professional experts earned their expertise by listening to their own Adrians, Beths, Dustys, and Chicorys. Harste, Woodward, and Burke (1984) advocate using the child as curricular and theoretical theorist and claim, "The use of the child as informant can become a self-correcting strategy for the profession" (p. 51). Hansen developed her ideas about the reading-writing connection through extensive research in classrooms. The Goodmans have studied the reading process for more than twenty-five years by listening to children and adults read orally.

As we as a nation struggle with the best ways to teach reading, we must recognize that Michelle is different from Marneka; Marneka is different from Nicole; Nicole is different from Paul; Paul is different from Adrian. Therefore, as Ed Fry suggests (cited in Flippo 1998), we must "Use a variety of methods." As George Spache says (cited in Flippo 1998), we must provide a variety of reading experiences, including vocabulary instruction, word analysis, phonics for some students, and comprehension instruction. We must also be ever vigilant with what Wayne Otto (cited in Flippo 1998) calls a "skeptic's stance" so that we are not taken in by heady claims of having the right answer. As

Rand Spiro (cited in Flippo 1998) reminds us, "Each paradigm for teaching reading and each theory of reading has strengths and weaknesses."

Since my early days of teaching, I have acquired a Ph.D. in literacy instruction from a "good" university. I have also had the privilege of having some other experts in the field as my mentors and friends—Rich Vacca, Nancy Padak, Tim Rasinski, Rob Tierney, and others. But I am always aware of the need to keep in touch with those experts in the classroom, the ones who taught me so much about reading and writing. Therefore, as Director of Curriculum and Instruction for a countywide Educational Service Center, I make sure I get into classrooms at least once every week. I have also learned that the most effective staff development I can organize is to invite panels of students to talk to educators about their learning. After one such panel, a principal said, "Imagine that. For twenty years I have been looking for the answer and it was right there under my nose all the time!"

The great rift over reading methodology that is harming our students will only be resolved when educators, legislators, and parents start listening to the experts such as the ones I had who taught me so much. Nancy Atwell (1987) says that "when we sit quietly, wait, and listen, our students will tell us what they're trying to do as [readers and] writers" (p. 63). We must listen to them. We simply have no choice!

References

Anderson, R.C. 1994. "Role of the Reader's Schema in Comprehension, Learning, and Memory." In *Theoretical Models and Processes of Reading: Fourth Edition*, ed. R.B. Ruddell, M.R. Ruddell, and H. Singer, 469–482. Newark, DE: International Reading Association.

Atwell, N. 1987. *In the Middle: Writing, Reading, and Learning with Adolescents*. Portsmouth, NH: Heinemann.

Brown, H. and B. Cambourne. 1987. *Read and Retell*. Portsmouth, NH: Heinemann.

Chall, J. 1967. *Learning to Read: The Great Debate*. New York: McGraw-Hill.

Durkin, D. 1978–1979. "What Classroom Observations Reveal About Reading Comprehension Instruction." *Reading Research Quarterly* 15 (4): 481–533.

Fawcett, G. 1990. "What Is Reading?" *The Reading Teacher* 44 (4): 349.

———. 1994. "Beth Starts Like Brown Bear!" *Phi Delta Kappan* 75 (9): 721–722.

Flippo, R.F. (1998). "Points of Agreement: A Display of Professional Unity in Our Field." *The Reading Teacher* 52 (1): 30–40.

Garner, R. 1994. "Metacognition and Executive Control." In *Theoretical Models and Processes of Reading: Fourth Edition*, ed. R.B. Ruddell, M.R. Ruddell, and H. Singer, 715–732. Newark, DE: International Reading Association.

Goodman, Y. 1978. "Kid Watching: An Alternative to Testing." *National Elementary Principal* 57 (4): 41–45.

Goodman, Y.M. and K.S. Goodman. 1994. "To Err Is Human: Learning About Language Processes by Analyzing Miscues." In *Theoretical Models and Processes of Reading: Fourth Edition*, ed. R.B. Ruddell, M.R. Ruddell, and H. Singer, 104–123. Newark, DE: International Reading Association.

Goodman, Y.M., D. Watson, and C. Burke. 1987. *Reading Miscue Inventory: Alternative Procedures*. New York: Richard C. Owen.

Hansen, J. 1987. *When Writers Read*. Portsmouth, NH: Heinemann.

Harste, J., V.A. Woodward, and C.L. Burke. 1984. *Language Stories & Literacy Lessons*. Portsmouth, NH: Heinemann.

Martin, B. 1967. *Brown Bear, Brown Bear, What Do You See?* New York: Henry Holt.

Ogle, D.M. 1986. "K-W-L: A Teaching Model That Develops Active Reading of Expository Text." *The Reading Teacher* 39 (6): 564–570.

Paris, S.G., M.Y. Lipson, and K.K. Wixson. 1994. "Becoming a Strategic Reader." In *Theoretical Models and Processes of Reading: Fourth Edition*, ed. R.B. Ruddell, M.R. Ruddell, and H. Singer, 788–810. Newark, DE: International Reading Association.

Paris, S.G. and M. Myers. 1981. "Comprehension Monitoring in Good and Poor Readers." *Journal of Reading Behavior* 13 (1): 5–22.

Pearson, P.D. 1993. "Teaching and Learning Reading: A Research Perspective." *Language Arts* 70 (6): 502–511.

―――― . 1994. "Reading Comprehension: What Works." *Educational Leadership* 51 (5): 62–68.

Read, C. 1975. "Children's Categorization of Speech Sounds in English." (Research Rep. No. 17). Urbana, IL: National Council of Teachers of English.

Stauffer, R. 1969. *Directing Reading Maturity as a Cognitive Process*. New York: Harper & Row.

Vacca, R.T. and J.A.L. Vacca. (1993). *Content Area Reading, Fourth Edition*. New York: HarperCollins.

6

My Experience as a Bilingual Teacher
Why I Agree with the "Experts"

Lilia Del Carmen Monzó

Building public trust in educators is of particular importance in California, where educational policy is increasingly enacted with little regard for the opinions of educational "experts" such as teachers, school administrators, and educational researchers. In 1995, the Board of Regents of the University of California, appointed by the Governor, voted to end affirmative action at the nine UC campuses in spite of vocal opposition from faculty and students (Epstein 1995). Not long after, the California legislature passed a bill requiring all students to take the same standardized test, the Stanford 9, regardless of English language proficiency, amidst opposition by school districts which publicly threatened to commit civil disobedience if the law was passed (Fernandez and Asimov 1998). More recently, Proposition 227 has banned bilingual education as we know it in California. A new "untested" model that will offer most students only one year of intensive English as a Second Language may soon go into effect. This measure also passed amidst significant opposition by school districts, teachers of bilingual programs, and other bilingual education experts (Asimov 1997, 1998).

Because the warnings of educators against unsound educational policy are not heeded, teachers are having to meet mandates that often go against what they know help students learn. For example, when and if Proposition 227 goes into effect, bilingual teachers throughout the state of California will have to forego the academic training that teaches them the significance of primary language instruction for the development of higher order thinking skills and for transferring these skills to the second language (Cummins 1984). They will have to teach students in English, even when they know their students do not have the English proficiency to understand content. They will have to conjure up ways in which to help build cultural pride and self-esteem while discrediting the prior knowledge of students because that knowledge is in a different language. Ultimately this lack of trust in the knowledge and experience of teachers will hurt students.

In order for educators to regain their "expert" voice in educational matters, the public must see educators as professionals that have a certain specialized knowledge. The numerous practices and contexts reported in this book that educational experts agree would facilitate and hinder reading speaks to the fact that indeed this core knowledge does exist and should weigh heavily on educational policy. As a teacher, this core knowledge of reading forms part of my own educational "expertise."

My Knowledge and Experience in Context

My knowledge of practices related to reading instruction comes primarily from my own teaching experience as well as from teacher education courses. I am a bilingual teacher and I have worked predominantly with working class Latina and Chicana communities in California.*

My teaching career began in 1991 in San Diego where I worked as a bilingual instructional aid and later as an on-site substitute teacher for a public elementary school located in Logan Heights, a very poor Latino and African-American community near downtown San Diego. The area was infamous among San Diego residents for significant gang activity. This position gave me the opportunity to observe a variety of classroom environments and numerous teaching practices.

Soon thereafter, I took my first "real" teaching position at a public elementary school in South Central Los Angeles where I taught in bilingual third- and fourth-grade classrooms for two years. The school serves an impoverished community whose average yearly income, at the time, was $4,000.00. As in other low income communities in California, intense poverty has given way to drugs and gang activity. Approximately 93% of the students were English language learners, primarily immigrant Latinas from Mexico, Guatemala, and El Salvador. A few were Chicanos, that is they were of Mexican descent but born in the United States. Some of these Chicana families have been living in the Los Angeles area for a number of generations.

I then moved upstate and took a position teaching first grade in a different type of bilingual program, a two-way bilingual, Spanish-immersion

*In order to minimize gender inequities in the text, I have chosen to alternate between the feminine version Latina community or Latinas and the masculine version Latino community or Latinos when indicating a plural that is inclusive of both genders. I have done the same with the plural of Chicana/o.

program. The school is a magnet school which means that it drew students from numerous communities in the surrounding areas. Latina families living in areas that did not offer bilingual programs traveled significant distances to place their children in this program.

The school is located in a middle-class urban community in San Mateo, California. Many of the Spanish speakers and a few of the English speakers were bused in from nearby low-income communities. I taught there for two years. The majority of my students were Latino and Chicano. Some were white. I had a few African-American students as well.

The communities in which I had previously worked were geographically segregated by race and class. As a result, I had not had the opportunity to compare, first hand, how race and class impact the education that children receive in schools. In this school, the students that were bused in from low-income communities had much in common with the students that I had worked with in San Diego and Los Angeles. In contrast, the students who came from English-speaking, middle-class families, whose parents had been successful in the educational system of this country, had greater opportunities. These parents often had the time, energy, and knowledge to prepare their children to meet the behavior and academic expectations of teachers.

As an immigrant Latina, working within my own ethnic and cultural community is very rewarding. It is also the community with which I can have the greatest impact. Many of the obstacles to educational success that Latino children now face are the same ones with which I once coped. Thus, my knowledge of what is most effective in teaching Latina and Chicana children also comes from lived experiences. For example, the issue of whether English language learners should receive instruction in their primary language is one that I feel strongly about because I know the day-to-day difficulties that students face when they are placed in classrooms where they do not understand the language that is spoken. I was placed in an English-only classroom although I spoke only Spanish. Not surprisingly I recall very little of my primary education. At the time my sister, who was a little older, recalls not being able to talk in school or understand what was being said for the first two years because she did not speak English. My parents, who did not speak English, were unable to communicate with my teachers or to help me with my homework. That is what Proposition 227 may bring us back to.

I have recently returned to Los Angeles and have been taking graduate courses at the University of Southern California, a private university located in South Central Los Angeles—not far from the school where I taught in Los Angeles. Interestingly, the university sits in what seems to be an island surrounded by poverty-stricken African-American and Latino communities.

Various projects have taken me as an observer to numerous classrooms in the area. I have had the opportunity to observe more experienced teachers and to learn from their reading instruction practices.

Core Knowledge: Concurring with the "Experts"

A Context for Reading

The "experts" as reported in this book agree that developing positive self-perceptions and expectations facilitates reading. Those of us who work directly with children know that providing an environment that supports this development is essential. Children do not all learn to read at the same time. For some children learning to read is a more difficult process than for others. Children who have positive self-perceptions are less likely to interpret reading difficulties as personal deficiency.

Children who have a positive self-perception are more willing to take risks (Page and Page 1992). This is very important because children learn to read by reading. I cannot teach students how to read without involving them in reading. This means that children must be willing to interpret meaning from print even before they can decode all the words. Thus, guessing and making mistakes are important parts of the process of learning to read.

Students who do not have a positive self-perception focus on what they cannot do and compare themselves with other students. Antonio, a Chicano first grader, was a very bright boy. He had good reading comprehension skills. He understood social studies and science concepts well and could explain them. He also did very well in math. Yet Antonio had difficulty accepting any help or suggestions for improving his work, such as letting me sound out words for him. His usual reaction was to put his head down and scream, "I can't do anything."

This negative self-perception seriously affected his reading and writing progress. Although Antonio entered first grade knowing the letter sounds, he did not experiment with reading or writing. As other students progressed in reading and writing and he did not, Antonio became ashamed. He began to refuse my help and the help of other students. Improving his self-perceptions was very difficult. I had to convince him that making mistakes was not an indication of intelligence or worth. It was not until late in the school year that Antonio began to feel proud of his accomplishments. This is when he began to make progress.

Children must also have positive expectations of what they can accomplish. This is especially important for children who experience difficulty with learning to read. Children who believe they will eventually be able to read strive for that goal by picking up books and writing at every opportunity. My experience has been that when students' improvements are not recognized they begin to think that they will never be able to read and simply stop trying.

My experience teaching a fourth-grade girl, Elena, to read exemplifies the importance of having positive self-perceptions and expectations. Elena entered our fourth-grade class about two months into the school year. When she arrived mid-morning, the class was working independently on writing an essay. After introducing her to the class, I gave her a bit of background as to what the class was working on and asked her to begin. When I was finished explaining, she looked up at me and said, "¡Pero maestra, yo no se escribir!" ("But teacher, I don't know how to write.") I was taken aback. After all, this was fourth grade. Certainly she should have learned, at the very least, concepts of print and some of the alphabet. She should have at least been encouraged to use written symbols and invented spelling to represent meaning.

I asked her to write her name for me which she did correctly, although with handwriting that looked as if she had had little experience with writing. Like the experts reported in this book, I knew of the connection between reading and writing, so I asked her to read a story for me. Again she said that she did not know how to read. I gave her the book anyway and asked her to try her best. She struggled, but as I guided her to use the visual clues, she got through the story. She skipped many words, used wrong tenses in others, but made sense of the print. I did not remark on the mistakes, but acknowledged her accomplishment jokingly saying, "I thought you said you didn't know how to read." I recall that Elena beamed.

Like the experts reported in this book, I knew that giving Elena any indication that I did not think she could learn to read would make learning to read difficult. Instead, I consistently made Elena feel that she was a reader and a writer. I continually acknowledged each of her improvements. Elena became an avid reader. Each day she would ask to borrow books so she could take them home to read. By the end of the year, Elena was reading "at grade level." The girl who had at one time felt she could not read or write had become a confident student who was motivated and tried her best not just in reading and writing, but across the curriculum.

Unfortunately some practices, such as ability grouping, expecting students to do it right or not at all, and "round robin reading," severely damage the self-perceptions and expectations of students. It is likely that some of these practices took place in Elena's previous classes. These are practices that often highlight what students can't do rather than what they can do.

In addition, these practices do not make sense in the context of a group learning environment. Because these practices put students' abilities on display, they make students vulnerable to teasing. They also encourage competition which the experts in this book agree makes learning to read difficult.

Ability grouping especially is difficult to manage in a group context. The result is differential access to a quality education (Mehan 1987).

Practices That Make Reading Difficult

Ability Grouping

The experts agree that grouping students according to ability makes learning to read difficult. It negatively affects the self-perception and expectations of the students placed in the "low" group. Even when every attempt is made to conceal the level of the group, students very quickly figure out which is the "high" group and which is the "low" group. This became quite clear to me early on in my teaching experience. My fourth graders could recite by memory the titles, in order from lowest to highest, of the reading books from the basal program in use. Furthermore they could tell you which was "appropriate" to which grade level. Clearly, then, students who were reading "below grade level" were well aware of the fact.

Even without such clearly leveled books, students can tell who the best readers are and who cannot yet read. My first graders were always quick to point out that Carlos, a Latino, was the best reader in the class. Many of the boys who could not read would often find their way to Carlos during silent reading so that he could read to them. Michael, an African-American boy who, although quite bright was not yet decoding, was cheered on by students the first time he came up to the board and read independently from our morning message.

Students range in reading ability. Knowing so is not a negative experience if students are taught that reading ability is acquired at different rates and that it is not an indication of intelligence or worth.

Unfortunately ability grouping gives a different message. Separating students on the basis of reading ability emphasizes the importance of the particular reading level. It gives little value to the improvement that students make in reading. Ability groups tend to be fixed for the entire school year, with very little mobility within groups. These are often the only groups to which students belong in the class. Since reading is often infused throughout the curriculum, the students in the "low" group tend to be thought of as the "low" students.

Students in the "low" group sometimes get teased. For these students, reading becomes a source of humiliation. In my experience, these students are less likely to enjoy reading and less likely to read during their free time or when they finish assignments early.

This emphasis on reading level is especially difficult for the population of students that I have worked with. Students from low-income families often do not have books at home. To reach the public library, students must walk through streets in which drugs are sold openly. Parents often work two and three jobs to make ends meet, leaving them little time to read with their children. In addition, immigrant families that I have worked with have a different understanding of how a parent helps their child to be successful in school, based on different cultural norms and a lack of understanding of how the educational system works in the United States.

These students are often at a disadvantage in comparison to students for whom reading is a daily activity. They are often labeled as "low" because they have had significantly less exposure to "mainstream" literacy activities and because their "funds of knowledge" go unrecognized (Gonzalez 1993).

Ability grouping tends to offer a very different quality of instruction to the different groups (Delgado-Gaitan 1989). In the schools I have worked in, I have observed that students rotate reading groups daily and thus each group is given an allotted time for each center which may be composed of a guided reading group, a writing activity, and some independent work (hopefully all related to a particular thematic unit). Each group should have an equal amount of time for reading. Unfortunately this does not work out well when students are grouped by ability. The "low" ability group often needs a greater amount of time to get through stories and still have enough time to discuss and do follow up activities. The result is often that the high groups have, on a daily basis, more time in their reading groups to devote to discussions that promote critical thinking. The low group usually has enough time to merely get through the story.

Furthermore, almost all of the "low" reading groups I have observed focus primarily on mechanical skills and phonics instruction. These are offered not in addition to but instead of lessons that promote critical thinking. Often the follow-up activities of "low" groups involve games that help students memorize sounds and letters or worksheets that narrow their thinking opportunities. In contrast, "high" groups tend to do follow-up activities that involve writing essays and stories. These are activities that allow students to be more creative.

Language-minority children, placed in English immersion classrooms, are often placed in the "low" reading groups because their literacy skills in their primary language go unrecognized. The basis for determining their reading level is pronunciation rather than comprehension (Díaz, Moll, and Mehan 1986). Since the emphasis is on their English language proficiency rather than their literacy skills in their primary language, these students are labeled as "Limited English Proficient" which implies a limitation and dismisses the importance of becoming literate in two languages. Furthermore, these low groups of English language learners are often taught by the teaching assistants who are hired as bilingual aids but who do not have the knowledge of pedagogy in reading instruction that teachers have (Ortíz 1988).

There is also some evidence that minority students, without regard to English proficiency, end up disproportionately assigned to the "low" groups

(Eder 1982). While I have not observed this first hand, a colleague once told me that in her first-grade class, her "lowest" readers were all Latinas. As teachers, we contribute to shaping the beliefs and perceptions of students. Are students informally learning, through ability grouping, that minority students are "low" students?

Doing It Right or Not at All

The experts agree that making sure that students *do it correctly or not at all* is a practice that would make learning to read difficult. I am also convinced, from my experience, that students who are consistently expected to do things "right" end up not taking risks for fear of not succeeding. When I taught third and fourth graders, I found that some students would try every excuse to avoid doing activities that they did not think they did well. In art, for example, some students often either asked me or the teaching assistant to do the drawing for them. The same was true for activities that involved reading. The students who felt that they read slowly or made too many mistakes decoding did not want to read out loud. I have often seen how students try to avoid being chosen by the teacher to read out loud. Some students hide behind classmates. Others sink low in their seats. Still others glance down and try to avoid eye contact with the teacher.

I recall one of my first graders who displayed an unusual nervousness while reading aloud. Juan was a good reader. He decoded well. When he made errors decoding he usually corrected himself immediately. He also had good reading comprehension skills and was able to retell stories after reading them. Yet when Juan read aloud he would try to speed up. Often he would skip words and change the endings of words. You could literally see sweat building up on his forehead. On the occasions in which we read aloud, one at a time, he always wanted to know when his turn was coming up and he would read ahead in order to be better prepared to pronounce the words correctly.

I spoke to his parents about the problem and the parents admitted that they consistently corrected him. They also told me that Juan's father was a perfectionist and very competitive. Juan's parents spoke to him, conveying that the most important thing was always to try his best and that he did not always have to be the best at everything. Although Juan continued to be competitive, he slowly began to read with greater ease.

Expecting students to read "right" or not at all can be disastrous. In order for children to learn to read, they must be allowed to read. Teachers cannot just show students how to read by reading to them. Students must also be given opportunities to read on their own. Thus, they will necessarily make many mistakes as they experiment with print in the process of learning to read. Beginning readers often skip words or use a different tense of the word in a way that makes sense to them. In writing they string whole thoughts together and skip letters and words. It is important to accept students' attempts at reading and writing. Giving them the impression that these mistakes are not a part of the process of learning to read and that they should be able to read correctly from the onset can negatively affect their self-perceptions and expectations. This does not mean that students should not be shown how to read and write correctly. Rather, they should be shown that the focus should be more on what they can do correctly than on the mistakes.

For example, in the first grade many students come in with very little experience with writing. Often they have never been expected to write anything but their name. When, on the first day of class, I pass out a journal and ask them to draw a picture and write about what they have drawn, their eyes open wide and most of them protest that they do not know how to write. They actually look terrified. I have even had a few students begin to whimper. The majority put down a few letters, maybe some numbers. If I do not accept what they have been able to do and I immediately correct them, they would be unwilling to try again the next day. Instead I indicate that even though what they have written may not exactly state what they want it to say, it is still good that they have written letters and have tried to write about what they have drawn. During these first weeks I continue to encourage them to write and I accept their early attempts. I help the students sound out words and encourage them to write down whatever sounds they hear. Slowly I point out things for them to improve on, all the while acknowledging what they have already accomplished.

A typical activity which fosters acceptance of the range of student abilities and promotes risk-taking behavior is the morning message that takes place in many first-grade classes. In this activity, the teacher writes a message and students come up and read whatever word or words they can glean from the message. Students who are not yet able to do this can give the sound of a letter or name a letter. This tells students that their development and accomplishments are each valued.

Unfortunately, these attempts by teachers to emphasize improvement and to allow students to feel good about whatever they can currently produce, is often sabotaged by state-imposed testing. These tests focus on whether students can or cannot find the "right" answers. There is little opportunity in these tests for students to demonstrate what they can really do. Often parts of the tests are well beyond the ability of even the more fluent readers. For those who struggle with reading, these tests do little but reinforce feelings of low ability and turn them off to reading.

I have had to administer these types of tests to first graders who finished the test feeling dejected. My students who were beginning readers struggled through the test. They seemed both scared and sad. It was as if all the progress they had struggled to achieve was for naught. The testing only reinforced negative self-perceptions which I had worked so hard to diminish.

For our language-minority students here in California who have to take standardized tests in English, it is all the more painful. When I had to administer the CTBS (now replaced by the Stanford 9) in the fourth grade, I recall that the students would look at me, silently asking for help. Yet guidelines for administering the test did not allow me to translate. For the most part students simply filled in the answer bubbles at random. I can only imagine how my students must have felt having to sit through a test in a language that they barely spoke. Whatever success they may have experienced in school that academic year must have seemed insignificant since they were unable to understand the test that they were being expected to take.

Demanding Correct Pronunciation

When working with the Latina community it is particularly important to accept the pronunciation that students use when they begin to speak and to read in English. If the student can be understood, correcting their pronunciation can be counterproductive. In my experience, the students who feel they have succeeded in speaking English are the ones who will continue to practice the English they are learning. This is especially true of older children who seem to be more self-conscious. During the years that I taught fourth grade, many of the students were very shy about speaking in English, especially in front of their peers.

When teachers consistently correct the pronunciation of English language learners who speak differently because they have an accent, they are informally teaching that there is something wrong with speaking differently. These students may begin to resent their culture and negate their ethnic identity. This could seriously affect their self-esteem (Phinney 1997).

One of the most disturbing stories I have heard as a teacher came from a parent. She had recently enrolled her first-grade son at our school. Fernando had entered my class approximately halfway through the school year. Fernando's mother is from Mexico and his father is from Puerto Rico. Both parents were raised in the United States and spoke fluent English. They were a middle-class family living in a community that was predominantly white and where the schools did not offer bilingual programs. Fernando was bilingual when he entered my class.

I met with Fernando's mother, Maria, after school. I explained to her that although Fernando seemed to be adjusting well with the children, he was very resistant to speaking Spanish. He often complained that he did not want to speak, read, or write in Spanish. He would become angry when I insisted.

Maria cried as she explained that Fernando had been attending the neighborhood school where all of the students were white and instruction was entirely in English. Fernando had stopped speaking in Spanish. He had been increasingly moody. One day she found him eating many white powder-covered donuts and spreading the powder on his face. He had explained to his mom that the kids at school always asked him why he was so dark. He had said he wanted to be white like the other kids and he did not want to speak in Spanish anymore.

Round Robin Reading

The "experts" reported in this book agree that "the practice of having one child at a time read aloud while the others follow along" makes learning to read difficult. They indicate that in this practice "students take turns going around the group in either a clockwise or counterclockwise manner." As a teacher, I have come to know this practice as "round robin reading." Through my own experimentation with the practice as well as multiple opportunities observing other teachers engage in this practice, I am also convinced that it makes learning to read difficult.

For the students that I work with, it is essential to utilize reading time in the classroom as efficiently as possible. Many of these students do not have books at home that they can read. The dangers of the streets where these students live make the public library difficult to access. The school libraries in the inner-city schools where I have worked have forbidden students to take the library books home because when these books are lost the families do not have the funds to replace them. Thus, my students have limited opportunities to read at home.

The key to helping students develop reading and writing proficiency is allowing kids to read at every opportunity in the classroom. Round robin reading wastes reading time. This practice offers each student only two or three minutes of reading time in a twenty-to-thirty minute reading slot.

Teachers who prefer round robin reading to other more independent reading practices assume that students are silently reading along with the student who reads aloud. What I have found, though, is that the students who should be following along often become distracted. They glance around the room or flip through the pages. Many of the students become bored and do not even listen to the reader so they also miss out on comprehension and the ability to use the comprehension for follow-up activities.

In my own reading groups and in observations, I have seen how students immerse themselves in their own reading when asked to read short guided reading books on their own. This always takes less time than reading one at a time and each student is engaged in reading the entire story. Since each child has read the entire story, discussions are much richer. Furthermore, reading becomes a source of personal enjoyment rather than a public demonstration of reading ability. More fluent readers can go back and reread while the slower readers can read at their own pace. In this manner, students are encouraged to read for meaning and comprehension rather than for speed and correct decoding.

For the beginning readers in my first-grade classes, previewing the book together then having a shared reading run was a good way to get them experimenting with reading the story on their own. Once they were ready to begin to experiment on their own, they tended to read aloud although not always in unison. The more fluent readers would help the others along, leaving oral reminders of the text that was to follow.

Round robin reading also has the negative aspect of putting student abilities on display. For students who may be less fluent decoders than others in the class, this can be a humiliating experience. "Slow" readers are often teased. Some students vocally complain that the student reads too slowly. Others brag that they already read the entire story silently while the reader was slowly decoding a small portion of the story. Although most teachers that I have observed will encourage students to be respectful to other students and discourage these types of comments, this cannot be entirely controlled. Often they are silent protests that take the form of loud sighs, rustling of paper as students stop listening and begin to read on their own, or whisperings to neighbors indicating that students have lost interest. The "low" reader who is put on display is left feeling inadequate and embarrassed.

During my first year teaching, I made the mistake of asking students to read aloud one at a time from their social studies text. Amalia, who had difficulty decoding, read very slowly. I recall the sighs of students who had to follow along with her and her downcast expression when she heard these sighs. I decided right then that this type of public display was unnecessary. It did not add anything to the students' learning that could not be added in other ways.

It is clear that this public display of ability is stressful to students. Even students in "high" groups will move ahead to read the section that they expect to have to read aloud in order to be better prepared to read it fluently when it is their turn. While doing this, comprehension of the story is lost. Practices that put student reading abilities on display give students the message that reading is primarily about decoding rather than extracting meaning from print.

Conclusion

Those of us who are educators, either teaching children directly or studying and investigating the best ways to teach children, have a specialized knowledge that is instrumental in providing students the best possible education. As I have tried to show, we know what works and what doesn't work in teaching.

Teachers often individualize instruction for each student depending on that student's specific needs. Many teachers in California are concerned that as politicians and others who do not have educational "expertise" begin to regulate the teaching and learning process into narrowly defined practices, the individual needs of students will not be met. These teachers express frustration and confusion over the increasing push to standardize teaching practices.

A clear example of how individualized instruction can have a significant effect on a student comes from a third-grade class that I observed regularly. I noticed that the Latina and Chicana girls in the class participated in classroom discussion very minimally and significantly less than other girls and boys in the class, with one exception. A Latina, Margarita, actually seemed to participate more often than anyone else in the class. She was always raising her hand to answer questions and to share ideas. The teacher, Ms. Martinez, also seemed to call on her consistently.

I asked the teacher about it and she explained that Margarita had entered her class the previous year. Ms. Martinez had been teaching second grade. Ms. Martinez said that, at that time, Margarita never once raised her hand to participate. Ms. Martinez would call on her to participate and Margarita would answer, but she would turn "red like a tomato."

The experts reported in this book agree that "listening, talking, reading, and writing should feed off of and into each other." Ms. Martinez understood this and knew that what Margarita shared in classroom discussions would be reflected in her writing and could increase comprehension of related readings. Furthermore, Ms. Martinez knew that the process of learning a second language would be faster if Margarita felt comfortable enough to practice speaking in English (Krashen 1982).

Ms. Martinez explained that she began to call on Margarita consistently, at first only when she was sure that Margarita knew the answer. Slowly Margarita began to feel a little less uncomfortable.

When Ms. Martinez found out she would be teaching third grade the following year, she asked to have Margarita placed in her class again. She continued to encourage Margarita's participation by consistently calling on her. Ms. Martinez said that her intervention had been slow but effective. Margarita had become a confident student who shared her ideas, asked questions, and took risks answering questions even when she was not completely sure of the answer. Furthermore, Margarita excelled in reading and writing in her primary language and was making significant progress in speaking, reading, and writing English.

References

Asimov, N. 1997. "Anti-Bilingual Plan Earns Ballot Spot: Educators Have Joined Forces to Fight English-only Measure." *San Francisco Chronicle*, 24 December, A11.

———. 1998. "Schools Try to Resist Bilingual Law." *San Francisco Chronicle*, 6 June, A1.

Cummins, J. 1984. *Bilingual and Special Education: Issues in Assessment and Pedagogy*. San Diego, CA: College-Hill.

Delgado-Gaitan, C. 1989. "Classroom Literacy Activity for Spanish Speaking Students." *Linguistics and Education* 1: 285–297.

Díaz, S., L. C. Moll, and H. Mehan. 1986. "Sociocultural Resources in Instruction: A Context-Specific Approach." In *Beyond Language: Social and Cultural Factors in Schooling Language Minority Students*, 187–230. Los Angeles: California State University, Evaluation, Dissemination, and Assessment Center.

Eder, D. 1982. "Differences in Communicative Styles Across Ability Groups." In *Communicating in the Classroom*, ed. L.C. Wilkinson, 245–264. Orlando, FL: Academic Press.

Epstein, E. 1995. "Faculty Opposes Gutting Affirmative Action at UC. They Want to Share in Decision-making." *San Francisco Chronicle*, 21 Oct, A13.

Fernandez, M. and N. Asimov. 1998. "S.F. School Board Flouts State Law." *San Francisco Chronicle*, 18 March, A15.

Gonzalez, N. 1993. *Teacher Research on Funds of Knowledge: Learning from Households*. Educational Practice Report: 6. Dialog, ERIC ED360 825.

Krashen, S. 1982. *Principles and Practice in Second Language Acquisition*, Oxford: Pergamon.

Mehan, H. 1987. "Language and Schooling." In *Interpretive Ethnography of Education: At Home and Abroad*, ed. G. and L. Spindler, 109–136. Hillsdale, NJ: Lawrence Erlbaum Associates.

Ortíz, F. I. 1988. "Hispanic-American Children's Experiences in Classrooms: A Comparison Between Hispanic and Non-Hispanic Children." In *Class, Race, and Gender in American Education*, ed. L. Weis, 63–86. New York: State University of New York Press.

Page, R. M. and T. S. Page. 1992. *Fostering Emotional Well-Being in the Classroom*. Boston: Jones and Bartlett.

Phinney, J. S. 1997. "Ethnic and American Identity as Predictors of Self-Esteem Among African American, Latino, and White Adolescents." *Journal of Youth and Adolescence* 26: 165–185.

7

Planning for Contexts and Practices That Facilitate Learning to Read

A Teacher's Perspective

KIM BOOTHROYD

Jodie stormed into the reading room one day, her face flushed with resistance, her eyes flashing, "Make me read, I dare you." For a six-year-old, in the middle of the first grade, she had a full plate. While her peers steadily gained in their literacy skills, Jodie slowly but surely lost ground. Jodie was her own worst enemy when it came to learning to read. She was thoroughly convinced that she would never read so she shut down with any activity that involved print. Where her strong will was working against her at the moment, in the future it would stand her in good stead when she began to accept and understand print.

For many kids reading arrives magically, seemingly without effort; for others like Jodie it can be a long, arduous process. In working with Jodie, her classroom teacher, her parents, and I did not look for any one approach that would teach her to read. We worked on the firm belief that all kids will learn to read. Working from what Jodie could do, we slowly built a reading program for Jodie that addressed her needs, as well as reinforced her strengths. We worked to combine many of the contexts and practices that the experts agree facilitate learning to read. Jodie is now in the third grade. She loves reading and writing, and, most importantly, she loves herself as a competent reader and learner.

In the last fifteen years, I have had the good fortune to teach in a wide range of classrooms, and to work with a diverse range of students, while implementing various reading methodologies and approaches. I taught in the inner city of Seattle, Washington, where I worked with pre-schoolers and first graders for five years using DISTAR (Carmine and Silbert 1978). DISTAR emphasizes phonics first as the foundation of the reading program. I relocated to central New York state where I taught second grade and fourth grade in a rural school that was immersed in literature-based instruction. Five years later, I moved to New York City to serve as the reading coordinator of an independent school in Greenwich Village. In this school, literacy instruction was based on a variety of methods and approaches to meet the needs, strategies, and motivations of different children. Now I am taking graduate courses in reading and writing at the University of New Hampshire.

Writing this chapter has provided me with an opportunity to reflect on my experiences while, at the same time, considering what it is that makes learning to read easy or difficult. My purpose in writing this chapter is to show the importance of planning for contexts and practices that promote learning to read. Planning is the foundation that facilitates learning to read and enables the instructional strategies and experiences the experts in this book advocate.

A Pre-Planned Program

Whatever anybody has told you about the weather in Seattle, it is true! It is a city surrounded by a multitude of environmental wonders: mountains, water, and deep forests. It is here that I began my teaching career. Although my students were primarily African American, a diverse array of energetic students attend Seattle public schools. The pre-school and first-grade classrooms in which I taught were not only filled with children from Seattle, but with children from Vietnam, Thailand, China, Japan, and Mexico.

I had been out of undergraduate school all of a year when I landed a job as a substitute teacher in a CAMPI pre-school classroom. CAMPI is an acronym for Central Area Mothers for Peace and Improvement. The central area in Seattle, at one time, had the highest minority population of any area in the city. The CAMPI program was developed by mothers from the central area, who wanted their children to have a chance for a better education. Initially, the pre-schools were set up in community centers and churches in the central district. The program was a part of Project Follow Through (Aukerman 1971).

There were two half-day programs with thirty-two four-year-olds in each program. The teaching vehicle was DISTAR (Direct Instruction Systems for Teaching Arithmetic and Reading). DISTAR was an intensive, fast-paced, highly prescribed program of instruction. It was developed by Siegfried Engelmann at the University of Illinois. DISTAR was originally intended for children from disadvantaged environments. (For more information about DISTAR see Carmine and Silbert 1978.)

Several years ago I realized that while some DISTAR methodology has stayed with me throughout my teaching career, I would not be comfortable using DISTAR again as my primary vehicle for reading instruction. What the experts in this book agree would make learning to read difficult are many of the same practices I struggled with when I used DISTAR. Literature was viewed as something apart from reading instruction, and writing took place in isolation. I found that the program focused on early mastery of the rules of reading, emphasized phonics instruction, and taught letters and words one at a time. Guessing was discouraged, feedback about errors was immediate, and all the kids were required to say the same sound, at the same time, correctly. To me this seemed more like military training than reading instruction. The experts in this book agree that ability grouping, an extreme emphasis on phonics, and "reading correctly" as the prime objective are practices that can make learning to read difficult. The students I worked with in Seattle learned to read phonetic readers, and, since standardized tests tend to emphasize decoding, their test scores improved. Everybody was pleased but me, because I knew we were only measuring a limited aspect of true reading ability.

I was new to the field, needed a job, and was excited just to be teaching. I did not ask too many questions, and I worked quietly in ways that filled in "the gaps" in the DISTAR program. I stocked our classroom library with literature. I expanded reading beyond the DISTAR reading group with literature extensions, theme projects, and meaningful writing. Yet DISTAR consumed a great deal of classroom time. In addition, behavior issues sometimes took precedence over instruction. Being a classroom teacher is always a juggling act. In many ways, my time constraints were the same ones most teachers face day in and day out. In spite of our DISTAR program, I worked hard to see that students engaged in purposeful reading and writing.

My Teaching Strategies

There were important teaching strategies I learned in those five years that had less to do with the content of DISTAR than how to manage numerous reading groups and structure a whole class reading program. The DISTAR program explicitly dictates each step the teacher is to follow while teaching reading. The format prescribed by DISTAR gave me the freedom to focus on the individual literacy needs of each student in my classroom. I did not focus on planning for reading groups because it was all done for me. I did not even have to think about what to say during reading instruction because DISTAR scripted it for me. DISTAR imposed a routine that I ultimately rejected, but, at the time, it allowed me to discover other aspects of teaching reading with young children. The time I would have spent planning became time to focus on reading as a functional tool for learning. In this way, I was able to develop positive self-perceptions and expectations for my students.

Even though I learned much about children as readers and worked hard to provide a rich literacy environment in Seattle, I think about the practices the experts suggest make learning to read difficult. Although my Seattle students learned to read and write, DISTAR did not make it easy for them. I taught reading at the same time every day. I grouped homogeneously and the reading groups usually consisted of four to six students. Group membership rarely changed and the kids always knew who the "poor" readers were. Additionally, I conducted all my small group instruction orally. As Flippo discusses the points upon which the experts agree, she explains why focusing on children's oral reading is not sound practice. When children are forced to focus on their own oral reading performance, they pay less attention to the meaning of what they are reading.

I also came to understand phonetic development during these years. This has helped me tremendously as a classroom teacher and a reading specialist. Understanding phonics instruction has freed me from the confines of a teacher's manual or a prescribed program. I discovered that I should know as much about the phonological development of children at all ages as I know about the best literature to share with them. Phonics plays a key role in children's ability as proficient readers, but I agree with the experts that emphasizing phonics instruction alone is not the best route to reading development. Children also need instruction in comprehension strategies and vocabulary.

As I review my teaching strategies, I recall that my Seattle classroom featured the typical calendar and schedule of the day on the board. Some bulletin boards displayed students' work; others centered on current themes or events. Students worked in small groups with me or read and wrote independently in a quiet spot in the room. Kids worked on a DISTAR worksheet or a literature extension at their desks or with a partner. Each student could tell you what they were doing and why. When I reflect back on my classroom and the literacy activities that took place, I realize that I never let go of the expectation that the children would learn to read. The experts all agree that it is critical to develop positive expectations for all students. Over the years I've been involved with different reading programs and methodologies, but I've always been guided by my expectation that students would eventually learn to read. Rahmel, a first grader I taught in Seattle, and Andrew, a second grader I later taught in central New York, come to mind when I think of students who succeeded because I never wavered in my belief in them as competent, capable readers.

Rahmel

Rahmel's eyes would well up with tears each time his reading group was called. He would be the last child to join us and the first one to dash back to his desk. This was not the wiry six-year-old I would often observe "ruling" the playground. He was quick witted and sharp tongued, and often I was the target of his words. Rahmel once told me he was to going to sue me if I did not stop trying to make him read.

I knew Rahmel would learn to read but he did not know that, yet. I never think for a moment that a student will not learn to read. He may need more time and different strategies, but, eventually, with the right guidance and instruction, he will read. It was a challenge to resist being drawn into Rahmel's arguments that he was not going to read. At the age of six he had learned numerous avoidance tactics. While I could not always find the words to convey to Rahmel that I knew he would read one day, I could create the environments and contexts that would help Rahmel discover reading as purposeful and meaningful. As Flippo reminds us, emerging readers need multiple, repeated demonstrations of what reading is and how it is used. DISTAR gave Rahmel the traditional skill and drill he needed but it was not enough.

Writing was Rahmel's ticket to reading. The more he wrote, the more his reading improved. I stumbled upon this when he began to write me notes about how mad he was at me. Rahmel came to enjoy writing notes to friends and family members. Initially, we privately reread these notes together. Eventually students in the class would ask Rahmel to help them decipher something they had written or had encountered in a book. The experts tell us that students need the time and opportunity to read and write purposefully. We can provide them with the time but if we do not expect them to read and write, many of our students will go through the motions but never feel the power and purpose of reading and writing. Rahmel had a real purpose and it gave him real direction. Rahmel was well on his way to becoming a reader and writer by the end of first grade!

A Self-Planned Program

One summer, just before I moved to central New York state, I received a phone call from Patti Farrell, the principal of my new school. She knew I would not be moving east until the end of August but she wondered if I would be able to meet with her as soon as I arrived. We met three weeks later. I knew I would be teaching second grade and I assumed that we would be discussing the beginning of the school year. Patti wanted to know if I would be interested in implementing a literature-based reading program in my classroom. I told her I would be very interested!

When school began that fall, I entered a new phase of reading instruction. In one fell swoop, I voluntarily moved to the opposite end of the reading spectrum as it has been portrayed by the media—an "either-or" approach to reading instruction (Flippo 1997). After working in a phonics-first program, I chose to implement a literacy program with a strong emphasis on real literature. We used literature to teach reading skills and strategies (including phonics) as well as to teach an appreciation for literature and reading.

Three key things happened in the years I taught reading in central New York, the first being the most important: I received administrative and parental support. I think that the experts who participated in "the Expert Study" would agree with me that the success of any reading program is incumbent on the support of administration and parents.

Not only did Patti Farrell support the transition I was making, she had a solid understanding of literacy development. As an administrator, Patti was guided by her clear vision of where the entire school community could go immersed in a program that used real literature for teaching. As important, she realized the transition could not happen overnight. She created a long-term plan: the first year one-third of the faculty implemented literature-based literacy instruction; the following year another third of the faculty made the transition; and by the third year, the remaining faculty was using literature as the primary tool for teaching reading. In this way, as a faculty, we could commiserate with each other and cheer each other on.

Patti was instrumental that first year in providing support for our entire faculty. We took classes, participated in workshops, and read the current professional literature. We also met twice a month to discuss what was working in our literacy programs and what was not. Similar support was in place throughout the duration of my employment in the school. The faculty and administration also held parent workshops, brought parents into the classroom, and welcomed parents in all ways into the school. It was, at times, a difficult challenge, but it was always exciting to teach reading and writing.

The second thing that happened when I was teaching in central New York is that I learned the importance of planning instruction and individual activities so that students engage in purposeful reading and writing. As the experts in this book agree, this is important! In Seattle, DISTAR robbed me of the opportunity to be an active professional literacy planner. As a result, my instruction was neither purposeful nor engaging. In central New York, as a teacher in the more empowering literature program, I carefully planned and organized my own classroom curriculum and instruction.

The heart of good classroom instruction is planning. In order to provide appropriate instruction, make learning purposeful and engaging for all the children in my classroom, careful planning was critical. I did not have a scripted curriculum to fall back on for any part of my day. I spent many hours each month mapping out plans. I believe that time spent planning gives more time for flexibility in the classroom. When I walk into the classroom knowing the plans for that day, week, and month, I can focus my energy and knowledge on the kids—which is right where it should be.

My long-term planning integrated reading instruction with social studies, science, and math instruction. I drew up "planning maps" that would cover three- to four-month periods of time. Often I planned with other teachers from the same grade level. From these planning maps I would break down planning further into weekly plans. By no means did these planning maps commit me to a plan that was inflexible; quite the opposite. As each day unfolded, the class might take a different direction based on something we read, a news article, an artifact a student brought into the classroom. But with a plan of instruction in place, I could prioritize and work in many of the interesting, but often unplanned learning opportunities that arise during any given school day.

Considering what to teach and when made planning sometimes feel like a three-ring circus. The school district required me to use four or more curriculums; math, science, social studies, and health, as well as reading, writing, and spelling. The students' interests and needs took precedence and I had interests I wanted to share with my students, too. I learned that one way to juggle all of this was to sit down with my students each month and plan together. I listed on chart paper what we had been learning, what I needed to teach based on district requirements, and then I invited my students to add their ideas. We discussed, debated, and prioritized our lists. I incorporated the lists into my planning when I taught second and later fourth grade in this school. Through our negotiation, I provided my students with responsibility and control over what they were learning. They saw that I valued what they had to say, and they had a choice in what they learned. Learning, whether it was reading, writing, or math, was meaningful for each student.

Andrew

Andrew Weld clung to his parents on the first day of school. He did not want them to leave his side and each time his mom tried to pull herself free, he wailed. Abby and Steve Weld were quiet, unassuming dairy farmers in central New York. They met while they were students in undergraduate school. After graduation and marriage, they decided to run Steve's family dairy farm and raise a family. Andrew is the oldest of three boys. Andrew wanted to be a farmer; he had no use for school and could not understand why his parents were forcing him to go. Part of me could not blame Andrew for not wanting to come into the classroom; the Weld family farm is an ideal setting for children. The farm features barns, a pond, horses, tractors, and acreage as far as the eye can see. School was the last place a seven-year-old farmer wanted to be. All teachers have Andrews or Andreas who unwillingly walk through our classroom doors every school year and challenge us to teach them. As the experts tell me, convincing Andrew that reading would help him become a better farmer was key to getting him through the door.

Not only did the students and I provide Andrew with a meaningful context for learning, Andrew brought the classroom together as a community. He taught me the invaluable lesson that learning is a transaction between the students, their families, and myself. As a teacher, I work hard to make reading meaningful for all my students. This is a Herculean task and not possible every minute of the school day or every day of the school week but it is a goal that is always on my mind.

The students in the classroom also contributed to meaningful learning experiences. Many of these kids had been with Andrew in kindergarten and first grade and provided me with a wealth of information about what Andrew liked and disliked. I combined his interests with his classmates' interests, and with the district's science curriculum for second grade and began the school year with a curriculum that centered on cows and dairy products—a bovine curriculum! We read nonfiction material about cows, as well as some trade books about cows and dairy farm life. We studied the digestive system of a cow which led us to investigate where milk comes from. I introduced the reproductive system of a cow and later in the year we would use the sample of that system as a comparison with the reproductive systems of other animals. We wrote narratives and developed research reports on cows.

Andrew became the class expert on cows. This young man might have difficulty with fluency, segmentation, and blending but he could enthrall seven-year-olds with his knowledge of the various breeds of cows. We created and tested recipes. The class went to the supermarket and got a listing of dairy products that we used for math activities. We went to the Weld's dairy farm where the class saw their bovine curriculum in action. Andrew no longer fought with his parents to get on the bus; he gladly came to school. The class worked with the bovine curriculum intensively for the first few weeks of school and gradually we moved on, referring back to it throughout the school year. More important, Andrew was convinced that reading and writing would help him learn more about becoming a knowledgeable farmer!

A Community of Readers and Writers: A Co-Planned Program

Nestled in a cramped four-story building in the center of Greenwich Village in New York City is the Little Red Elisabeth Irwin School where I taught for five years. Four-year-olds through ten-year-olds fill the lower school, middle schoolers take up the adjacent building, and the high school is a few blocks away. I was the reading coordinator for the lower school. My primary responsibilities were to attend to the literacy needs of all students whether they were struggling or successful readers and writers. In addition, I met weekly with classroom teachers to plan, talk, and discuss reading and writing. I also conducted the assessments and evaluations, and did admissions intakes in the lower school. I was busy but I was never happier as a teacher.

Reading and writing were not just about what *I* brought to the classroom or what *I* thought a child needed; we worked as a team. Literacy instruction, planning, and implementation was coordinated and overseen by me. However, the faculty, staff, specialists, students, parents, and administration made the success of the reading program possible. There were frequent planning meetings, daily check-ins with classroom teachers as well as consistent communication between home and school. I spent the first half-hour of the morning, before the start of the school day, talking with each classroom teacher. I was revisiting and discussing what the teacher and I would be doing for reading and writing that day. Although each teacher and I had planned reading instruction together the week before, touching base with teachers ensured that we were always working together on literacy instruction. We were consistently working towards supporting our students' literacy efforts. Often these check-ins took no more than two minutes; yet it was the daily communication with faculty and staff, whether we were talking about a student or seeing if there were any changes in plans, that increased the effectiveness of our reading program.

This school's philosophy was to fit the curriculum to the child not the child to the curriculum. This philosophy is not always viable every moment of the school day. However, in the daily life of a classroom, in small and meaningful ways, fitting the curriculum to the child is consistently possible. Schools can create literacy programs that meet the needs, strategies, and motivations of different children at different times and in different situations. The administration of this school provided teachers with the professional latitude to select procedures, methods, and approaches that were appropriate for each particular child in each particular context (Flippo 1997).

This was a school with limited financial resources. Families who came to this school did so because of the philosophy of the school not because of the school's elaborate facilities. The faculty, administration, and parents developed and built a community of readers and writers. A similar community can be created in any school, public or private. Studies show that good teachers know what their students need; as a result, teachers do not implement any one specific instructional program (Pressley, Rankin, and Yokoi 1996). Flippo reminds us that the intention of her study was not to prescribe any one method or approach but instead to learn what contexts and practices, as recommended by reading experts, best facilitate reading development. There is clear evidence that there is no one technique or procedure that is best for all students when it comes to learning to read and write. Instead, the experts value classroom contexts and practices that help children develop an awareness of the interrelatedness of oral and written communication because these processes are so intertwined.

Teaching students to read is not just about phonics or literature. The planning that created the reading program in our Greenwich Village school, as well as the work by the classroom teachers, the specialists, and administrators, are what account for our students' literacy gains. I now see literacy instruction as a sound collaboration between reading, writing, talking, and listening that can build a community of readers in any school. The experts confirm this for me.

The entire faculty of the Little Red Elisabeth Irwin School was highly invested in reading, writing, and learning. The specialists, school psychologist, and administrators met weekly in the lower school with classroom teachers to plan instruction and discuss students. Our planning was collaborative. In the weekly planning meetings I had with classroom teachers, we would discuss and plan for the following week's reading instruction. We would discuss various students, work and rework the skills we were introducing, and review the literature we planned to use. We were not working on teaching isolated skills separately from the context and content of our classrooms; instead we worked in conjunction with the classroom teachers and the specialists to plan for skills instruction within our classroom contexts and content.

In Retrospect

It is exhausting to be a teacher; our students challenge us with a wide variety of learning needs. We are not likely to create the contexts and practices that support learning to read just by opening a teacher's manual and reading what comes next. Jane Hansen writes about the importance of a community of readers and writers (Hansen 1987). In New York City, I learned that in order to build a community of readers in our classrooms, we also had to build a community of learners in our schools—administrators, faculty, and staff who all worked together to support each other in teaching our students. I would never say, "This is my reading program," nor could anyone else at the Little Red Elisabeth Irwin School. The reading program was developed by the entire lower school. Typical of many schools in which I have worked, the faculty did not always agree with administration or with each other. Developing a solid literacy program is challenging and time consuming. There is no one right way.

Reading instruction in this school was based on an inclusion model where students with learning needs stayed in the classroom as much as possible.

Groupings of students changed frequently. Groups were formed based on on-going assessments and teacher observations. In a first-grade classroom, the classroom teacher might chorally read a big book with half the class while the associate teacher would work with a small group on skill instruction. At another table, I might work with another small group on a word identification activity. Other children would be off in quiet corners of the room reading silently.

In a second-grade room the students studied the motifs that can be found in fairy tales. They read a variety of traditional and modern fairy tales. Several times throughout the year, as kids read silently, the classroom teacher and I would go from student to student having them read orally to us while we made notations about the miscues they made as they read. We used this information to plan lessons over the next few weeks.

In a third-grade classroom, students analyzed books about Christopher Columbus comparing facts from the books to facts they have discovered as they study explorers. Over on the rug, two kids worked on a research report on Marco Polo. In a fourth-grade room the class read memoirs at the same time they were writing their individual memoirs. During reading workshop, the classroom teacher shared her current draft of her memoir and asked students for their feedback. In all of these examples, the students were engaged in purposeful reading.

Final Reflection

The stories of the beginning readers in this chapter illustrate the importance of creating contexts and environments in which all children can learn to read and write. Jodie was a student at the Little Red Elisabeth Irwin School in New York City, Rahmel attended an inner-city school in Seattle, Washington, and Andrew went to a rural school in central New York. Each child's literacy development combined elements that make learning to read possible. This chapter showcases what can be accomplished when teachers work together with administration, staff, and students, remain sensitive to the unique needs and experiences of their students, and pay attention to the recommendation of the reading experts as they create a solid literacy program. In the midst of the whole language versus phonics debate, we can find reassurance in the findings of Flippo's Expert Study which suggest to me that a philosophy of balanced literacy instruction facilitates reading development.

References

Aukerman, R.C. 1971. *Approaches to Beginning Reading*, 2nd ed. New York: John Wiley and Sons.

Carmine, D. and J. Silbert. 1978. *Direct Reading Instruction.* New York: Merrill Publishing.

Flippo, R.F. 1997. "Sensationalism, Politics, and Literacy: What's Going On?" *Phi Delta Kappan* 79 (4): 301–304.

Hansen, J. 1987. *When Writers Read.* Portsmouth, NH: Heinemann.

Pressley, M., J. Rankin, and L. Yokoi. 1996. "A Survey of the Instructional Practices of Outstanding Primary-Level Teachers." *Elementary School Journal* 90: 251–274.

8

Teaching Children to Read
It's Harder Than You Think

MARGARET BERRY

Since I became a first grade teacher, many friends, acquaintances, and parents often ask me what must seem to them a simple question: "How do you teach children to read?" I know they are hoping for some quick yet astute answer that would sum it all up. However, it's just not that easy. Instead, I usually ramble on until they must wish they hadn't asked in the first place.

If they can get a word in during my long explanation, they try to shorten my answer by asking: "Do you use phonics or that new thing?" This one proves somewhat easier for me because I always say "both," an answer that must be as annoying as my long one. For me, however, answering that question does little to answer the first. And, both questions show how many people expect an easy answer to the question of how we teach reading.

They do so in part because many in the media, some politicians, and many others discussing the issues surrounding reading fail to portray it as the complex process it is. In fact, they insinuate that teaching reading is so simple that if we teachers would only choose the right method or follow a particular program, all the reading problems of the world would be solved. Some have even made it seem that teachers are not even that necessary; teaching reading is such a rote task that a computer could do it. But, anyone who has ever attempted to teach a room of twenty-two children with diverse backgrounds, interests, and abilities to read knows better.

Teaching reading is a complex and difficult task. Accordingly, like most teachers, I do not spend much time considering how to categorize my lessons, activities, or approaches. Instead, I try to figure how to make the best use of a very limited amount of time to make children lifelong, capable, confident readers. If a lesson or activity seems likely or has proven to help children in that process, I will use it. I do not reject or choose lessons or ideas by looking at whether they have been labeled as whole language or phonics. Instead, based on research, the experiences of other teachers, my own experiences, and to some extent, common sense, I work with my team to create a balanced program that accomplishes that goal. Our program changes constantly as we find things that work better, discard activities or books that do not seem to be working, and address new problems or questions that arise.

The first thing I noticed and appreciated about Rona's study and the statements on which her experts agreed was the extent to which they inherently valued and acknowledged the complexity of what reading teachers must do. The range of dimensions measured in the statements reflected how much effort, knowledge, and skill contributed to a successful reading program.

Second, the statements on which the experts agreed show that the alleged divide between so-called phonics advocates and those supporting whole language is not nearly as wide as many, particularly those in the media, would have us believe. Instead, there is much on which good reading teachers, no matter to which perspective or philosophy they subscribe, agree. And many use the same lessons and approaches no matter how they might label themselves philosophically. While obviously there are many differences as well, it seems so much more positive and helpful to reflect on what unites teachers, not what divides us.

As I read the experts' statements, I saw much of what we have tried to do in our own reading program reflected in them. I want to focus on several of them which we have found essential in our own efforts to teach reading:

1. Develop positive self-perceptions and expectations.
2. Make reading functional and create environments, contexts in which the children become convinced that reading does further the purposes of their lives.
3. Organize your classroom around a variety of print settings, and use a variety of print settings in your classroom.
4. Give your students lots of time and opportunity to read real books. Likewise, give your students lots of time and opportunity to write creatively and/or for purposeful school assignments.
5. Provide multiple, repeated demonstrations of how reading is done and/or used.

While none of these factors alone will "teach children to read," I have found that a classroom where they are integral parts is one where most children successfully learn to read and to love reading. Accordingly, I want to address each of them briefly and describe both why and how I try to accomplish each.

Develop Positive Self-Perceptions and Expectations

It is interesting how differently we treat the successes and failures of children who are learning to speak from those of children learning to read. We celebrate every little sound that comes out of babies' mouths, rejoice over their first words, and marvel when they begin to put those words into sentences. In contrast, we worry over every little mistake and miscue the beginning reader makes.

I have an eleven-month-old nephew who recently said "mama" for the first time. My sister was so excited, but, when he did not say it again for weeks, she did not panic or worry that her son was never going to learn to speak. Instead, she just assumed that someday soon he would begin saying "mama" regularly. Of course, he did. In the meantime, she enjoyed his many other utterances. While perhaps disappointed that he began saying "da" for "dog" before he regularly said "mama," she remained confident in his overall abilities.

Our reactions to children who are learning to read are so, so different. At every misstep we worry that our children will not learn to read. We do not have the patience we have for beginning speakers either, as we become easily frustrated when reading with beginning readers. Parents communicate these frustrations to me all the time:

> "I don't understand it. He just read the word on the page before, and he has forgotten it by the next page."
>
> "I tell her to sound it out but by the time she gets to the third or fourth letter, she gives up."
>
> "He does not really read. He just memorizes books and looks at the pictures."

And, it is not just parents. There have been so many times when I have been reading with a child, and he or she stumbles on a word which seems so easy that I just cannot understand how he or she does not know it! For example, last fall I was reading *Cookie's Week* (Ward 1988) with a child. It is a predictable book in that every page follows this pattern: "On [day of the week], Cookie [had some misfortune]. There was [result] everywhere." Prior to my reading with the child, the class had read the book as a group several times, and we had even written our own versions of it. Nonetheless, when I read with the child, he could not figure out the words "there was." Page after page, I would finally just have to tell him the words, and I found myself, embarrassingly enough, feeling quite frustrated with him.

While obviously we need to know what children's weaknesses are in order to address and remedy them, we also need to focus more on what they are doing correctly. Even children who cannot "read" in the traditional sense of decoding words often know and daily demonstrate quite a bit of knowledge about reading. For example, children who "only" read books that they have memorized or who use the pictures to read are showing, among other things, that they understand the way books in our language begin at the front and go from page to page thereafter, that stories are supposed to make sense, and that the words somehow relate to the pictures. These are important understandings that provide a good basis for learning to read.

As parents and teachers, we need to celebrate these beginning successes as much as we herald the first words and utterances of our babies. When we see a child using a specific strategy, like skipping a word and returning to it, or demonstrating some other knowledge about text, we should point out that accomplishment and praise him for it. Despite my occasional failure to do so, an integral part of my job as a reading teacher is to look for the good in children's reading and point it out to them.

Moreover, I have to work on lessening the anxieties about reading that children bring to first grade, whatever their source. One way I try to do that is to discuss specifically, at the beginning of the year, the meaning of developmental differences and how every person learns various skills and concepts at different times and in different ways. The children and I graph when they learned to talk and to walk. When the children's parents can remember, we also discuss what the children's first words and first sentences were—children are always delighted and amazed at the range of differences among them and among what they all first said. Some started with the simple "mama" while others spoke in nearly complete sentences from the beginning. Finally, I discuss with the class how everyone is talking and walking now and how those early differences have little impact on their current speaking abilities. Although these and the many other exercises in which we engage cannot completely alleviate children's anxieties about whether and when they are going to learn to read, they definitely help.

Like many teachers, I also spend considerable time at Parents' Night and other times trying to teach parents how to look for what is good in reading. I compare learning to read to learning to speak and encourage them not to worry if their first grade child is not remembering words from page to page or is having trouble with various sounds and certainly not to convey those worries to children. I also give them examples of early successes for which to look. Similarly, when I get phone calls from anxious parents, I do the same. Nothing can unsettle a child more than knowing that a valued adult has doubts about whether she is ever going to learn to read. Hard as it may be, we have to rejoice in the accomplishments beginning readers make, rather than focusing too heavily on their failures.

Making Reading Functional and Creating Environments, Contexts in Which the Children Become Convinced That Reading Does Further the Purposes of Their Lives

I am always amazed at how many people in the "reading wars" have discussed reading in such bloodless, simplistic terms as if teaching children to decode words is our only job. They seem to say that if we simply teach children the sounds and how to put the sounds together to make words, our job will be finished. But, couldn't anyone do that? And would children who had become perfect decoders also automatically become good readers who read for life?

The answer is no. I found that out my first year of teaching when I taught two students who had been "reading" since age three. They could decode virtually any text they encountered. They amazed and entertained adults with that ability. But, they often neither understood nor enjoyed what they were reading. It was not until the middle of second grade that they actually began to see books as exciting and engaging and reading as a worthwhile activity for themselves. Decoding was not all they needed to be taught.

Our job as reading teachers encompasses much more than teaching decoding but instead requires that we instill in children such a desire to read that long after they leave our classrooms, they will be reading books, engaging in literate discussions, and recommending books to friends. Last year a former parent came by my classroom to tell me that her child never went anywhere without a book; he read on the way to school, he read while they waited during his brother's piano lessons, he was constantly on the look-out for new books. This, not a child's score on a test or ability to decode a passage correctly, is the kind of feedback for which a first-grade teacher works.

To become lifelong readers, children have to see books and print as interesting, important, vital aspects of their everyday lives. They also have to learn to comprehend what they are reading as they are reading. Ultimately, they have to learn to question what they read: Is this book a good story? Is this factual account accurate or believable? Is this book fact or fiction? These and many more factors make children want to read for life, and I have not succeeded if I have not put them on the path of becoming people who want and need to read for the rest of their lives.

Making Books Seem Interesting, Important, and Vital

Making reading seem fun and exciting for first graders requires picking books and materials that I love and enjoy. I often find that my excitement about a book or unit is infectious and greatly influences how students react. For example, in my first year of teaching, another teacher introduced me to Cynthia

Rylant's Henry and Mudge series (for example, *Henry and Mudge, The First Book of Their Adventures* 1987). I loved the books' simple stories about real life experiences, the charming illustrations, and the way the series developed the relationship between Henry and his dog Mudge. My class loved them too, and we spent several weeks reading the books, writing our own versions, writing letters to Henry and Mudge, and drawing pictures of the characters. That year, I just so happened to get a puppy, and of course, my class insisted I name him Mudge. I did, and the Henry and Mudge unit has become a first-grade institution; by the time the class has heard all the adventures of my own Mudge, they are dying to read the Henry and Mudge books. Many "learn to read," in the sense of becoming fairly fluent readers, during that February unit.

In the spring, we have a fairy tale unit which also motivates and excites many beginning readers. We begin the unit by reading many versions of Cinderella, traditional versions, versions from other countries, and funny versions such as Alan Schroeder's *Smoky Mountain Rose* (1997), Frances Minters' *Cinderelly* (1994), and Susan Meddaugh's *Cinderella's Rat* (1997). There is something for everyone in all these versions. In fact, by the time I have read *Smoky Mountain Rose* in my best Southern dialect, children are practically fighting over the book, dying to be the first to read it for themselves. Tying the fairy tale unit to social studies, we also put a fairy tale character such as Goldilocks on trial, studying both the fairy tale and the jury system. During this unit, children become so excited about fairy tales, reading as many as they can and creating wonderful written work related to them.

There are also times when following the children's interests is necessary for building up interest and excitement about books. A few years ago I had a class that was virtually obsessed with mysteries. If I had ignored this interest, I would have sent a message that their interests were unimportant, that school reading was somehow different from real reading. So, I planned a unit on mysteries, using Marjorie Sharmat's *Nate the Great* books (for example, *Nate the Great* [1972], the first book in the series) as a base, and taught reading and its concomitant skills through that. For me, using real books of interest and excitement for children and planning engaging activities around those books are the only ways to generate the kind of enthusiasm about reading that will make children lifelong readers.

Even when focusing on specific skills that may be necessary for children to become good readers, I try to use meaningful materials and activities that make the skills seem relevant. Being able to fill in worksheets on the "sh" sound may or may not reinforce children's knowledge of that sound, but it will not make them want to read words with those sounds. However, teaching the "sh" sound in the context of a funny story like *Mrs. Wishy-Washy* (Cowley 1980) will.

Teaching Decoding and Comprehension in Tandem

Teaching children to comprehend what they are reading as they read is another vital aspect of making them lifelong readers. This is but one of many reasons why I feel that solely teaching phonics will not produce readers who want to read and who will do so for fun and for information. When my niece was in kindergarten, her class used a fairly structured, sequential program for teaching reading. The books they read used very controlled vocabulary. Each night she was to read a different book. One night we were reading one that was working on teaching the "an" sound. It seemed that every other word ended in "an," such as "The man ran to the fan. The fan was in the pan." As we were reading, she stopped and said, "I just don't get these books; they don't make any sense." As she labored through them, phonics was the only strategy she had to decode words, and reading was neither fun nor interesting. It has taken her a few years to recover from these books and look at reading as fun, not work. While some children who learn through this process may well become lifelong readers, why make any of their reading experiences negative, unpleasant, or unproductive?

That is not to say that children do not need to read levelled books that roughly match their current reading abilities. However, even in choosing these books, I try to pick ones that have some meaning or appeal for children. Audrey Wood's book *Silly Sally* (1992) is one such book. It is fairly simple in its choice of words:

Silly Sally went to town, walking backwards upside down.
On the way, she met a dog, a silly dog. They played leapfrog.

In addition, the book contains incredibly rich pictures, entertaining depictions of the characters and hints about what will happen next. It is the kind of book that children want to read again and again. I can then use it to teach many skills. For example, by cutting up the words in its simple sentences, mixing the words up, and having children put the sentences back in order, I am able to teach one to one correspondence. Similarly, the book is rich in sight words on which we work. Children who use books like *Silly Sally* to learn to read are learning not only that reading involves figuring out the words but also that it entails getting the message, the humor, and the fun of the text itself.

I do not want to imply that using fun, interesting books and making reading exciting alone will lead to a successful reading program. Of course not. However, building such excitement and enthusiasm are necessary components of one. If we want reading to become part of children's lives, we have to make them want to read.

Organize Your Classroom Around a Variety of Print Settings, and Use a Variety of Print Settings in Your Classroom

Although perhaps a more mundane topic than creating excitement about reading, setting up a print-rich classroom has also proven remarkably important to children's learning to read. The classroom should be full of words and opportunities to read, just as the home is full of much speech and many opportunities for babies to speak.

Having an interesting and diverse classroom library is probably the most important aspect of creating a literate classroom environment. I try to have books at many different levels, of many different types, and of many different genres. I also attempt to organize all these books to reach the greatest number of children. Many reluctant readers do not like to spend a lot of time searching for a book. For them, I use upright bookcases and my window sills to display interesting books on whatever our current topic of choice is, including my own books or ones I have gotten from the library. I also have bins containing fairly simple books through which students can flip as they look for ones that fit their current reading level. Further, I try to group popular authors or series books together; for example, there is a Clifford box (containing, for example, Norman Bridwell's *Clifford the Big Red Dog* [1963] and other Clifford favorites) and a box for books by Ezra Jack Keats, one of the authors we study in first grade. I organize the rest of the books alphabetically, by the author's last name, because there are always quite a few children who enjoy going through these books, looking for something new and exciting. To make reading seem a functional, important part of children's lives, I have to have books of interest to everyone and a way for all children to find reading materials they like.

Another key part of our classroom library are books that the children have written and published. In fact, depending upon the author or the subject, children frequently vie with each other as to who is going to get these books. The authors themselves take great pride in being able to file their books according to their last names and in seeing their friends check out their works.

I also have many references to the alphabet and its sounds available. We have a wall chart with the alphabet, as well as individual alphabets on each student's desk. In addition, each child has an index card with a small version of the alphabet which contains a picture clue for the sound or sounds that each letter makes. While some children entering first grade no longer need such explicit alphabetic references, many others do. Especially at the beginning of the year, I see children referring to these alphabet charts and cards again and again as they try to read through a book or write.

Children also learn a lot from their names and the names of their friends. Accordingly, I try to label everything with their names at the beginning of the year and to use their names in lessons near the beginning of the year. For example, in one lesson we sort our names in many ways, such as according to the beginning letter, the type of vowel sound contained in the name, or the number of syllables. I actually learned about the benefits of using names from my students. During our spelling time, I often found that as I introduced a new sound or spelling pattern, children would automatically refer to a friend's name that contained that sound or pattern. Having their names all over the room, playing games with those names, and using their names in various pieces that I write all reinforce the natural associations children make with their own and each others' names.

Similarly, beginning with the first day of school, I label everything within the context of the classroom with one label a day. It becomes a game for children to find the new label every day. However, as children search for it, they learn and practice many reading skills. Not only do they have to read over many of the prior labels but they have to figure out what the new label says. Later in the year, I switch to Spanish labels, which provide a whole new set of challenges.

Whenever we read a poem as a class or create a chart as a class, I leave those up for display so that children can read them again and again. It is sometimes difficult to find enough wall space for all the poems and charts, but it is worth the effort. I often see children re-reading the poems or referring to the charts, either just for fun or to glean some needed information. For example, each year the children make calendars as gifts for their parents. Before we start those, we create a class chart of each month and various holidays or activities for that month. Later, the children can often be seen referring to that chart, trying to think of a theme or picture for a given month.

Although perhaps less substantive, I also try to have word puzzles and word games available around the room and as part of the curriculum. We start the year with hangman, move onto scrambled words, then to analogies, and finally, to crossword puzzles. For some children these puzzles are very motivating and a fun way to learn new vocabulary and word identification skills.

The classroom also contains communications, letters we have received from others, notes I write to the children, notes they write to each other, and notes they write to me. For example, like many teachers, every day I write a message to the class as a whole about what we will be doing that day, especially highlighting unusual events or what our enrichment classes will be. I also write many individual messages, perhaps leaving a note for a student in his journal or writing a note about something that another student needs to finish. Children often write me notes as well; for example, a child recently wrote to tell me that he wanted me to change his desk location because he could not see from where he was sitting. Although it sometimes becomes hard to respond to all these notes, I try. Children find these personal communications very motivating, and they want to be able to read them.

There are obviously many other ways to create a classroom rich in print. Whatever ways a teacher chooses, it is important for children to have a room that is stimulating, inviting, and full of things to read.

Give Your Students Lots of Time and Opportunity to Read Real Books. Likewise, Give Your Students Lots of Time and Opportunity to Write Creatively and/or for Purposeful School Assignments

Just as children cannot learn to speak without lots of opportunities to try to talk, make sounds and so forth, children cannot learn to read and write without devoting lots of time to those activities. While this may seem like a fairly obvious point, there are many constraints at work that keep teachers and students from having that kind of time during the day. It is a constant battle to make and maintain enough time and opportunities for reading.

These constraints come from many sources both external and internal to the classroom. Externally, much school time is used for activities such as class pictures, visitors to the school, and enrichment classes like physical education, art, and music. While it should go without saying that these and many more required activities have considerable merit of their own, they nonetheless take away from reading activities. There is not much teachers can do about these.

However, teachers do have control over other incentives that they face and that lessen the time available for reading and writing. One of those incentives comes from the need to manage large groups of children; to have time to work with small groups or children individually, teachers have to have something for the remaining children to do. Without careful choices, those activities can quickly become mere "busy work." At the other extreme, in our efforts to make school a fun and interesting place and to integrate many subject areas into the curriculum, teachers often develop units which, while accomplishing those goals, involve more making and building than reading and writing. Resisting these temptations becomes one of a reading teacher's most important duties.

For me, it has been a struggle to avoid both extremes. When I first started teaching first grade, I used a "center" approach. I read with one group of children while four other groups had an assigned activity to complete. Many of these activities were relatively easy or rote activities. After a few months, I became uncomfortable with this approach. The work children did at these times was not particularly good, and I knew that I was not particularly concerned with the purpose for these activities. I was assigning "busy work." I started looking around for other ways to continue to have time for reading with children individually or in small groups but also to have the other children more actively and meaningfully engaged than they had been previously.

After much research, thought, and discussion, our first-grade team accordingly developed "literacy choices," a menu of activities for the week from which students can choose during their independent work times. The choices for the week usually relate to a particular theme or book we are studying. For example, during our fairy tale unit, we were recently reading multiple versions of *The Three Billy Goats Gruff* (Dewan 1995; Galdone 1973; Stevens 1987), and students who were not working with me or my assistant had a choice of the following extension activities:

1. Make a storyboard and puppets for *The Three Billy Goats Gruff*. Act it out for the class or in private for the teacher.
2. Write a letter to the Three Billy Goats from the Troll.
3. Make a map of the area where the story of *The Three Billy Goats Gruff* takes place.
4. Write a letter from the Third Billy Goat to the Troll.
5. Pretend you are a troll. Write about why trolls are better than goats.
6. Pretend you are a goat. Write about why goats are better than trolls.
7. Make a comic book version of *The Three Billy Goats Gruff*.
8. Write a new version of *The Three Billy Goats Gruff*, but use characters other than goats and trolls, such as "The Three Porky Pigs Puff."

In selecting choices for the week, we try to make sure there is an identifiable and valuable purpose, which relates to reading and writing, for each menu choice. Moreover, we try to make sure we include choices over a range of levels, from very simple choices, such as making puppets and a storyboard to retell the story, to more difficult ones, such as writing a new version.

The way in which students have responded to these choices and the quality of the work they have produced during that time have exceeded whatever expectations we might have had for them originally. For example, in connection with *The Three Billy Goats Gruff*, one student wrote a letter from the troll to the goats in which she said, "All righty there, maybe you think you got out of this. WELL, you didn't because I've got me some lawyers, you stinky goats." Another student wrote this list of reasons why billy goats are better than trolls:

Goats have horns. Trolls don't. Billy goats are clean. Trolls are dirty. Billy goats rule. Trolls drool. Billy goats are stronger than trolls. Trolls are weak. There are more goats than trolls.

Through such wonderful, meaningful writings, children have shown me that during the hour of time when they are working on literacy choices, they are engaged in purposeful reading and writing.

While these students are engaged in literacy choices, other students are receiving more direct instruction in reading or writing from either my assistant teacher or me. During these reading times, I group children either according to their current needs, according to interest, or randomly, depending upon my purposes for the week.

During these small group times, I select books that both relate to the theme we are studying and match the current reading needs, purposes, and interests of the group. Before we read, we preview the pictures in the book for clues to predict its subject matter, and we also review strategies we should use as we read through the book. Students then read the book. Afterwards, we discuss its meaning and purpose, usually through questions I have planned in advance. We also engage in some skill-related activity. The activities widely vary, depending upon the book or the goal or objective for a given reading period. For example, after reading Ezra Jack Keats' *The Snowy Day* (1962), we discuss the word "snow" and how "ow" sounds like long "o" in that word. Students then generate other words that end in "ow" and sound like "snow."

In addition to these structured reading times and lessons, I try to build reading and writing into many other aspects of the day. When students enter the classroom in the morning, they have to answer a brief question, such as, "Do you like pepperoni pizza?" Students then look for clips with their names and answer "yes" or "no." As a class, we then use their answers to this question to figure out our attendance for the day, including how many people are present and absent and who is absent. We also use it to explore various math concepts such as whether more people answered "yes" or "no" and how many more people answered one way or the other. While this is a small and quick activity, it is very meaningful for students. They take great pride whenever they can read the attendance question all by themselves. When they cannot do so, I often see two or three students studying the question together, suggesting ways to figure out unknown words.

As mentioned earlier, I also write the class a morning message about what we are going to do that day. While I read this message aloud during calendar time, many students try to read it on their own before I do so. Again, I see and hear them using strategies we discuss during more structured reading lessons.

Calendar time itself provides other reading opportunities. The calendar board contains structured sentences in English and Spanish about the date, such as "Today is Monday, March 22, 1998." At the beginning of the year, one student uses a pointer to point to each word while other students volunteer to read aloud. Later in the year, when this activity becomes too easy, we drop it from our calendar routine, but at the beginning of the year, it is a great way to build sight word recognition for some easy words and to teach one to one correspondence. During calendar time we also often do a quick word puzzle or game.

At the end of calendar time, we also read poetry or sing. Poetry, with its patterns and rhymes, is a natural way for children to learn to read. It lends itself to memorization, and it naturally encourages children to look for patterns in words. Shel Silverstein's "The Mummy" (1996) is a perfect example of such a poem, and it is amazing to see how many children can recognize the words "toilet paper" after we have read that poem many times.

After this calendar time, I model some particular writing skill through a mini-lesson in which I write in my own journal. For example, I have recently been modeling how to plan and write stories with an identifiable beginning, middle, and ending. When I engage in such group writing, I look for ways to encourage students to read as I write—I might use their names in the story I am writing so they quickly become attuned to what I am writing, or I purposely make mistakes that they are eager to correct. In any event, this quick time often provides many meaningful opportunities not only for children to read what I have written but also to learn the particular writing skill on which I am focusing.

Then, students write in their journals. They can write whatever they like, from personal narratives to stories. Sometimes we also use this time to write letters to classroom visitors or some other person with whom we have been communicating. During this 20–30 minute time period, I can meet with children individually and focus on particular needs that they have in their writing. For example, recently a child was using "h" indiscriminately for "ch," "sh," and "th." During journal time, we made a card with picture clues to help her distinguish better among the three sounds.

After our journal time, we do some large group reading activity. Sometimes I just read aloud to the group. Sometimes we discuss some particular aspect of the book. At other times, we focus on a particular reading strategy. For example, often I encourage children to skip a particularly hard word and return to it after reading a little more of the sentence. To work on this skill, I choose a big book, cover up certain words in it using cover-up tape, and ask for students' ideas about what the word might be after we have read the whole sentence. During this reading time, we also sometimes write class books, usually a new version of books we have read. Students then can take these books home to read with their families. They are quite popular, and they provide another way to reinforce the message that reading is a fun, social activity.

These morning literacy activities create several hours of time in which students are specifically and meaningfully engaged in reading and writing. In addition to this morning time, each day I read aloud from a "chapter book" to the class. We also have 20–25 minutes of sustained silent reading during which the children can read books of their choosing. While it is often an effort to make sure we get this time in every day, it is well worth that effort.

Without time to practice their burgeoning skills, students would not learn to read and write. We have to fight all the forces that take away from this time and create many meaningful opportunities for children to read.

Provide Multiple, Repeated Demonstrations of How Reading Is Done and/or Used

What makes reading such a complex process is that there is no one strategy readers can use to decode words which will work every time. Our language does not follow strict rules and patterns, and reading itself is such a complex activity that no one strategy will work. Moreover, different strategies work well for different people. Some children have such a good knowledge of the context of stories that they can read many books relying on that contextual knowledge; others are more keyed into the way words work and do better by sounding out words. In any event, reading and readers are too complicated to teach only one strategy.

Accordingly, we try to teach, model, and choose books that require many different reading strategies. Among other things, we model and teach children to sound out unknown words, to divide longer words into parts, to think of another word that they know and which resembles the word they are decoding, to make an educated guess based on context, to look at pictures, to skip the word and return to it, or to use a combination of these strategies.

We can model and teach these strategies using even very simple works of children's literature. For instance, although fairly easy, Frank Asch's *Just Like Daddy* (1981) calls for readers to use many diverse strategies:

> I washed my face, got dressed, and had a big breakfast.
> Just like Daddy.

Children can sound out many of the simpler words in this passage such as "got" and "big." However, there are also several words in this section that do not follow the rules of phonics as we teach them. Most children cannot sound out "washed" or "breakfast" accurately. Nonetheless, if they are taught also to use context and picture clues, or to read ahead and come back to difficult words, most of them can easily read this passage.

We teach parents these various strategies as well. In discussions with some parents, I have learned that the only advice they offer their children when reading with them is to tell them to "sound it out," advice which sometimes proves completely ineffective. Parents are often relieved to learn other ways to help their children read unfamiliar words.

Of course, among the many strategies we teach, we do teach children to "sound out" words. In fact, we work extensively not only on learning various sounds and combinations of sounds but also on how to put those sounds together to make words. But, this is only one of many strategies. Students who rely too heavily on sounding out words cannot read effectively. Moreover, reading becomes too hard for them. After they labor over every letter of every word, they are naturally tired and may not even have thought about a book's meaning.

Children need to learn that there are many ways to figure out unknown words and that good readers use a variety of ways. Both during the large group reading lessons and the small guided reading ones, I try to model, teach, and practice with the children many strategies for decoding; we also often discuss these explicitly before we read.

Conclusion

So, how do we teach children to read? Probably no one can give the succinct answer we all would like to this question. However, as Rona's study has shown, the experts agree on many contexts and practices which benefit children who are learning to read. Implementing those contexts and practices may be difficult, but it is such a worthwhile and rewarding adventure. Every time a child becomes excited about a book, reads a "hard" book for the first time, or overcomes some other obstacle on her way to becoming a lifelong reader, I am reminded of why I have chosen this career and what an honor it is to be a teacher. It is a feeling I am sure I share with many other teachers, no matter what their perspective or philosophy.

References

Asch, F. 1981. *Just Like Daddy*. New York, NY: Half Moon Books.

Bridwell, N. 1963. *Clifford the Big Red Dog*. New York, NY: Scholastic.

Cowley, J. 1980. *Mrs. Wishy-Washy*. Auckland, New Zealand: Shortland Publications.

Dewan, T. 1995. *Three Billy Goats Gruff, or 3 Strikes, Yer Out!* New York, NY: Scholastic.

Galdone, P. 1973. *The Three Billy Goats Gruff*. New York, NY: Clarion Books.

Keats, E. J. 1962. *The Snowy Day*. New York, NY: Puffin Books.

Meddaugh, S. 1997. *Cinderella's Rat*. Boston, MA: Houghton Mifflin.

Minters, F. 1994. *Cinderelly*. New York, NY: Viking.

Rylant, C. 1987. *Henry and Mudge, The First Book of Their Adventures*. New York, NY: Simon & Schuster.

Schroeder, A. 1997. *Smoky Mountain Rose*. New York, NY: Dial Books.

Sharmat, M. 1972. *Nate the Great.* New York, NY: Bantam Doubleday Dell Books.

Shaw, C. 1947. *It Looked Like Spilt Milk.* New York, NY: Scholastic.

Silverstein, S. 1996. "The Mummy." In *Falling Up.* New York, NY: Scholastic.

Stevens, J. 1987.*The Three Billy Goats Gruff.* New York, NY: Harcourt Brace and Co.

Ward, C. 1988. *Cookie's Week.* New York, NY: Scholastic.

Wood, A. 1992. *Silly Sally.* New York, NY: Scholastic.

9

A Synthesis
The Study and the Lessons

The last four chapters have been written by experienced and gifted, yet very different school practitioners, working in different areas of the United States with varied populations of students. Each of them has offered her unique perspective on how the findings from the expert study are meaningful to her own classroom experiences and learnings.

Analyzing and synthesizing their voices has been both a delightful and rewarding experience for me. In this chapter I discuss their sharings and synthesize their wisdom. Next, I focus on what I learned from their expert sharing, and finally I summarize the need for teachers and other school professionals to be more vocal in "the debate," advocating for continuing the conversation and using it as an opportunity for professional reflection and development. Following this chapter, I invite you to join in and participate in this process.

But first let's review the contributions of the school practitioners.

Gay

Gay Fawcett, an experienced classroom teacher and currently a curriculum director in Ohio, shares her classroom understandings and insights. Gay begins by telling how *she had no choice* but to learn from the little "experts" in her classrooms during her first and subsequent years of teaching.

Her little experts taught her a lot. Similarly to the experts reported by my study, Gay's "experts" provided tremendous insights into the teaching and learning process. The insights provided by them came, of course, from her astute observations of how they each learned to read best.

Then Gay artfully weaves her own experiences and understandings with those of other experts, citing many from my study for their special teachings and research. Her own insights reflect the growing understanding on the part of the entire reading literacy field over the years and are exemplified in her carefully selected examples of learnings from her own little experts.

Gay advises all of us who are concerned with reading development never to lose sight of the individual children with whom we work: They are each uniquely different, and what works with one may not be right for the next one. She reminds us that there can be no single answer or method. Answers must be found on an individual basis. Different answers will be right for different children. Rather than seeking universal answers, we must instead observe and listen to what individual children show and tell us about their reading. Because, as she explains, *we really have no choice!*

Lilia

Next, Lilia Del Carmen Monzó, a Los Angeles bilingual teacher, shares her insights from various inner-city schools she has worked in, first as a bilingual instructional aide and then a substitute teacher in a very poor Latino and African-American community in San Diego. Later she taught a combination of third- and fourth-grade Latino and Chicano students in another very poor community, this time in South Central Los Angeles. In the San Mateo bay area she taught first-grade Latinos and Chicanos in a magnet school located in a middle-class white community. Many of her students were bused in from surrounding low-income areas. There she could observe differences between children who had been nurtured by parents who were successful and who better understood the educational system of the United States and those whose parents had not received the benefits of that system.

Lilia shares her own immigrant roots and makes a case for children being taught in their own language. She discusses the legislative decisions recently made in California affecting bilingual teachers and learners. She points out how these decisions were made in spite of the protests by educational "experts" (teachers, school administrators, and educational researchers alike). She asserts that in order for school professionals and researchers to regain their "expert" voice in educational decision-making, the public must begin to see educators as professionals who have specialized knowledge. She believes that the agreements from this study indicate that a core of specialized knowledge of reading does exist, and she shows how some of the agreed-upon practices have taken shape in the classrooms where she has spent her time.

Lilia shares her classroom insights that support the "expert study" findings with examples of her experiences with Latino, Chicano, and other minority children and their parents. She presents reasons, for instance, why so many minority students are labeled and put into "low" reading groups. She explains how unfair and disheartening it is to use standardized tests in English to evaluate the reading and other academic accomplishments of students whose English proficiency is limited.

Lilia also describes inner-city community situations where access to books and other print is almost nonexistent outside of school; where going to public libraries means walking through dangerous and drug-infested neighborhoods.

She asserts, finally, that *teachers like herself know what works and what doesn't work in their classrooms.* She fears that as politicians and others without this expertise continue to regulate and narrowly define teaching practices, the needs of individual students will not be met.

Kim

Then Kim, a teacher who has taught in classrooms ranging from pre-school through fourth grade, from one side of the United States (Seattle) to the other (New York City), recounts her experiences with very different programs and children.

Kim began her teaching career in inner-city Seattle, teaching many young children from East Asian cultures (Vietnam, Thailand, China, and Japan), as well as a predominantly African-American population. The early childhood program she worked with had adopted DISTAR, a highly scripted, phonics-focused program. She explains that many of the DISTAR practices fit the description of contexts and practices that the experts in my study agreed would make learning to read difficult. She felt that the instruction she was made to provide more resembled "military training" than reading instruction.

Kim did what many teachers have had to do when faced with rigid rules that limit their instructional approaches: *she "went underground!" whenever possible.* She did the best she could to fill in the gaps so that at least some of the time her young students were engaged in purposeful reading and writing.

Kim's next teaching position was in central New York state, where she taught second grade and later taught fourth grade, using a literature-based reading program, a tremendous transition from the phonics-based program she had been using in Seattle! Kim reflects that the success of the program was greatly facilitated by the strong support received from both the school administration and the children's parents. Likewise, parents were always made welcome and were viewed as an important part of the school.

During this time, Kim learned the importance of planning and reflects that it was empowering to be treated professionally and allowed to plan her own instruction. She likewise passed some of this empowerment over to her students, involving them in curriculum choices and planning as much as possible.

Finally, Kim describes her years in a private Greenwich Village school in New York City as reading coordinator of a program for four- through ten-year-olds. This school valued each and every child's individuality, and once again, Kim was in a place that provided her with the professional latitude to plan for each child and situation. She thrived in this professional environment!

Kim is convinced that when teachers, staff, and administration work and plan together with sensitivity to the unique needs of their students, a powerful learning community develops. A balanced philosophy of literacy instruction, she believes, facilitates reading development.

Margaret

Last but by no means least, Margaret, formerly an attorney and now an experienced teacher in Nashville, Tennessee, enlightens us with her discussion of the agreements and what she does as a first-grade teacher. Margaret does not try to simplify her role as a teacher of reading because she knows it isn't simple. She tells us right away: *it is harder than you might think!*

Reading is a complex process and Margaret clearly recognizes this. Margaret tells us that no matter how often people ask for them, there are no easy answers about how to teach reading. Instead, she talks about *using what works* with children. She is interested in teaching them to read and develop into life-long, capable, confident readers, regardless of whether an activity or approach has been labeled as whole language or phonics or anything else.

Margaret focuses on several of the agreements that facilitate reading development, highlighting and reflecting on those that she has found through her experience most important to children's success. She touches on many other of the agreements, pointing them out along the way. She provides examples of what she does as a teacher to nurture these successes and selectively shows how good stories and children's literature enhance her instruction and the excitement of reading for children. For instance, she tells how in her first year of teaching she introduced the Henry and Mudge series books to her first-graders. The children loved them. They read all the books in the series and later wrote their own versions. Children wrote letters to Henry and Mudge and drew pictures of the characters. Then, later in the year when Margaret got a puppy, the children begged her to name him Mudge. That year and since, Margaret has excited children with stories of the real Mudge and his adventures. Although Margaret doesn't say it in her chapter, I'm certain that children also write, illustrate, and share many of the real Mudge stories in her classroom.

Margaret reads a lot of interesting and motivating books to the children. She explains that after these readings children cannot wait to read these books themselves. For instance, she tells how, by the time she has finished reading *Smoky Mountain Rose* (Schroeder 1997) in her best Southern dialect, the "children are practically fighting over the book." (And I believe it!) She uses children's interests to help select books to share. Margaret uses these books to cultivate the children's enthusiasm and at the same time *teach specific skills* in context.

Margaret provides many opportunities for writing in her classroom. She ties writing in with reading. Children are excited about the books they are reading, and Margaret encourages them to write and share their own books. Their authored books have become an integral part of the classroom library.

She also believes in empowering children and giving them "choices" over their reading and writing activities. These "choices" are carefully planned by Margaret to provide rich opportunities for rewarding, purposeful, and meaningful reading and writing.

Additionally, Margaret clearly does believe in instruction in reading skills. She provides many powerful examples of how she develops alphabetic knowledge, cultivates phonemic awareness, teaches phonics, and teaches other word identification as well as contextual strategies in her classroom.

She is clearly an artful teacher. She teaches because she loves it. She has developed her expertise through both experience and great insight into children and what will make them want to read. Margaret considers herself *a reading teacher* first. She uses that description of herself in many places in her chapter, and she teaches reading and writing as part of everything she does with children. Descriptions of her classroom context and practices are inspirational. I am certain that motivation and engagement must be very high in her classroom.

Margaret ends her chapter telling us with pride the honor she feels at being a teacher: telling us, too, that *she ultimately chose teaching because she knows how very important it is.* After reading her chapter, we all know that this is true. I've always believed that when teachers have pride in and enjoy what they do, feel professional, and are likewise treated as knowledgeable professionals, they will do their finest work. Margaret and the other expert practitioners who have contributed to this book are prime examples of this.

What I Have Learned

The expert teachers contributing to this book agreed with the judgments of the professional experts on many of the same points reported in my study. As I analyzed the beliefs and stories of these teachers, I noted that, overall, although the different teachers emphasized different points of agreement, there were some agreements in particular that all or at least most had strong feelings about.

One agreement especially stands out. Each of the teachers made it very clear that "*developing positive self-perceptions and expectations*" *is vital to facilitating learning to read.* This should be no surprise to any of us. These expert practitioners, just like the professional experts in my study, *know* the importance of children's self-perceptions and feelings of self-worth.

They also know and have shared with us the importance of "*creating environments and contexts in which children become convinced that reading does further the purposes of their lives,*" and "*giving students lots of time and opportunity to read real books*" and "*write for purposeful school assignments.*" These practices, they know, lead to increased motivation and engagement, which lead to higher reading achievement.

They have shown us, too, that "*repeated demonstrations of how reading is done and used*" are highly important. These are models of the reading process that students can emulate. The teachers in this book have provided this modeling by reading and sharing engaging books, stories, and other literature with the children entrusted to them.

These expert teachers have all shown that they value "*combining reading and writing,*" "*planning instruction so children engage in purposeful reading and writing,*" and "*using every opportunity to bring reading, writing, talking, and listening together*" (rather than teaching them as something separate) in their classrooms.

Finally, they too have made it clear that "*drilling children extensively on isolated letters and sounds*" is a practice that would make learning to read difficult. In fact, Margaret pointed out examples of children who can correctly sound out and pronounce all the words in a story, but who still do not comprehend or enjoy reading it.

The Culture of the Classroom

Strickland and Cullinan (1990) talk about the culture of the learning environment. They indicate that when the skills of written language are embedded in the very culture of the classroom, reading and writing will develop (p. 429).

I suggest that this literacy-valued culture and environment are one of the most important commonalities shared by the expert practitioners who have contributed to this book. Each teacher has clearly articulated classroom cultures that strongly value literacy. Children are given many and multiple opportunities to learn about literacy, appreciate literacy, learn the skills and strategies of literacy, and learn to consider themselves as literate individuals. And they do learn!

These teachers use methods, approaches, and strategies that they have found to successfully promote a highly literate culture and environment in their classrooms. They use what *they know* from their experience with each child will work best for each child. They have created classrooms where reading and writing, and using reading and writing, are part of everything that goes on. In other words, reading and writing have become major dimensions of the culture of each of these teachers' classrooms.

As you later consider and react to the experts' agreements, consider also the classroom culture that these agreements imply.

Print Access and Literacy Opportunities

Obviously, providing children access to print goes hand in hand with classroom cultures that put a high value on literacy. However, print access and literacy opportunities are not universally common and not universally available or equal for all children outside the classroom. As Lilia has pointed out, many children do not have interesting and stimulating reading materials to read in their homes; and getting to a public library is not necessarily easy or even safe for many of these children. Furthermore, school libraries restrict children from taking library books home if they believe the children can't afford to pay for books that are lost or damaged. Access to print and many literacy opportunities in the classroom are therefore that much more vital for these children.

Research has clearly supported the importance of print access and literacy opportunities. Morrow (1992) found, for instance, that increasing minority children's access to books in classroom libraries and teacher-guided literature activities led to more reading and higher levels of reading achievement. Elley's (1994) analysis of the 1992 international study of reading in 32 countries indicates that, among other things, *reading achievement is greater when students have access to good books*, when they enjoy reading and they read frequently, and when their first language is the same as the language of the school.

McQuillan's (1998) extensive review provides further support for the importance of print access and its relationship to reading achievement. Overall, children who have an opportunity to read more, read better. In fact, he suggests that because print access is so important, it makes good sense to judge instructional methods by examining the amount of meaningful print they expose children to (pp. 60–61).

Finally, Coles (1998) has shown the strong relationship between poverty, social status, and print access. What Lilia shares in her chapter confirms this.

The teachers who contributed to this book all know the importance of print access. A review of their chapters indicates that each one of them uses methods, strategies, and approaches that frequently expose children to meaningful print. Additionally, each one of them clearly makes print access and literacy opportunities a top priority in their classroom programs! Their experiences provide practical confirmation that print access and literacy opportunities make a real difference.

The Strengths of Relying on Teachers

As Calfee (1996) suggests, in his discussion on assessment, the classroom teacher is in the best position to assess students (p. 248). Likewise, I have learned that the classroom teacher is *also* in the best position to make decisions about instruction for children (Flippo 1997). Certainly, no outside person, group, or board could possibly know better than Gay, Lilia, Kim, or Margaret what instruction and assessment approaches and strategies are best for Beth, Elena, Rahmel, or one of the other children in their classrooms. *These teachers clearly have the expertise to know what is best!*

Gay suggests that she had no choice but to learn from her little experts. I maintain that *we really have no choice but to learn from all our teachers!* As pointed out in the next section, no amount of mandates will really change teacher beliefs, values, and practices in the classroom. The teacher expertise that I observe, from reading Chapters Five through Eight, demonstrates to me the insight and wisdom of practitioners who love to teach, know their students, and feel professional.

If, on the other hand, we fail to place our trust in teachers and rely on them, denying them the respect due them as professionals, then we will lose a very potent dimension of teaching success: a teaching force who are enabled to do their finest work because they are empowered, respected, and feel professional. This is one of the real strengths of relying on teachers.

The Weaknesses of Mandates and External Controls

One of the weaknesses of mandates and external controls is that they simply don't work. For instance, we remember how Kim, when faced with using a scripted reading program consisting of very little real reading (DISTAR), went "underground" and quietly used other materials and teaching strategies that *she knew* would engage her students in purposeful reading and writing. Kim *knew* that DISTAR wasn't enough. Her students needed more than an emphasis on decoding instruction. Kim couldn't be controlled to teach as she was told. No teacher can.

Allington and Walmsley (1995) also indicate that classroom literacy instruction cannot be significantly improved by issuing mandates or tightening the controls on classroom practices. They say that available evidence suggests that most teachers work hard at doing what they know. No amount of external pressure or controls can make teachers more expert in their classroom work (p. 261).

Another weakness of mandates and controls is that they cause ill-will. No professionals want to be told what they should or should not do. No teachers, administrators, or other school professionals who have worked hard, prepared themselves professionally, and made every effort to know their students and their motivations and needs will happily accept being controlled. If, as we know, these mandates and controls don't work, why impose them only to create ill-will?

A major weakness of mandating and trying to control what goes on in classrooms is that it disempowers teachers. We have seen evidence, in the four chapters authored by the expert teachers in this book, of what wondrous results can come from teachers who are empowered to teach as they know best. I could not imagine Gay, Lilia, Kim, or Margaret disempowered. They are experts at what they do, and they do it *so* well! And they are just a sample of the many, many other wonderful teachers and other school practitioners who every day work so very hard weaving their magic with children and doing what they know and do best. What possible advantage could there be in disempowering our teachers?

A related major weakness is that mandates and external controls can critically wound *both teachers and children!* Teachers' feelings of professionalism, the respect of others, and freedom to make instructional decisions, allow teachers to do their finest work with children. If wounds and controls go deep enough, some teachers might lose respect for their school systems or for their state education authorities. These teachers may decide that they cannot or do not want to teach any longer. After all, if their hands become completely tied and they can no longer openly weave their magic with children, some teachers may decide that they can't effectively teach or just don't want to be in their classrooms any longer. We can lose wonderful teachers! And the future reading development of our children will be affected. (Can you imagine the loss to the children if Gay, Lilia, Kim, Margaret, and others like them were no longer involved in classrooms?)

Reading is a complex process, and mandated quick-fix solutions and external controls are not likely to solve anything. In fact, they are more likely to create a whole new slew of problems—like motivation, disenfranchised teachers and learners, and children who will go to school without having their individual needs met.

In Summary

Many teachers are doing a wonderful job in our classrooms. They know what they are doing and why. *They know* how best to teach children and how to meet their needs. These teachers should be encouraged to continue to do what they do so very well. And for those teachers who could do better, mandates and external controls will not make them better teachers. These teachers need *professional* development and *professional* nurturing, *not controls.* Teachers like Gay, Lilia, Kim, and Margaret can be entrusted to work with teachers who will accept and welcome professional nurturing.

Additionally, as suggested in some of the sections that follow, professional discussions, reflections on the contexts and practices discussed in this book, self-study, and continuations of related conversations should also be very helpful to teachers who want to further professionalize their knowledge, skills, and strategies. But, as suggested here, this professionalism should be self-imposed, coming from within each teacher, not externally dictated, or it just won't work.

Our professional experts (in my study) and our teacher experts (in this book) have told us what contexts and practices they believe, based on their varied and extensive research and experience, would make learning to read difficult, and what contexts and practices would facilitate learning to read. Additionally, as pointed out in Chapter 4, other research supports these experts' agreements. We do have some common ground. We do have some agreement.

But more is still needed. In summary, I suggest that teachers and other school professionals need to be more vocal and involved in "the debate." *Teachers are experts* in their own right, as demonstrated by Gay, Lilia, Kim, and Margaret.

How Can Teachers Participate More?

Right now I can think of at least three ways teachers can participate more:

1. Talk to parents, families, and other community members who know you and respect your expertise. Tell them *what you know, how you know it,* and *why it is so important and vital to their children's future as lifelong, purposeful, active readers.*

2. Discuss "the expert study" and explore the issues that come forward in your local paper and from your state boards of education and school systems with your colleagues at grade-level and faculty meetings. (More on this in the section that follows.)

3. Participate in the follow-up study to share your agreements regarding contexts and practices for classroom reading. (See the invitation to participate and the response form following this chapter.)

Continuing the Conversation

Use opportunities for sharing and continued conversation as a vehicle for professional reflection and development.

Each of the practitioners who contributed chapters to this book told me that doing her chapter gave her a chance to really think about, focus on, and reflect on what she believes and knows about children's reading development. This opportunity for self-study and reflection could also be helpful for many other teachers and school professionals. Self-exploration, sharing, and "continuing the conversation" could in fact be a wonderful way to promote both professional knowledge and professionalism.

For instance, teachers and other school professionals could be encouraged to share experiences from their classrooms and school practice. Sharing could include role-playing, written or verbal reflections, debates, and other exploratory activities. Additionally, opportunities for selected readings and discussion groups to further explore specific contexts and practices, and issues or concerns, would all promote professional knowledge and growth.

I suggest that use of the expert study findings together with exploration of local issues and selected and pertinent questions could serve as a stimulating series of topics for professional development discussions and sharings at grade-level, building-level, and staff meetings.

Accompanying questions could include:

1. What do we know about our children's motivations for reading and writing?
2. What might enhance their motivations?
3. What might hinder their motivations?
4. What classroom environments would provide our children with a context to maximize their opportunities to read and write?
5. How can a school and a teacher best assess and evaluate children's literacy development, growth, successes, and needs?

Teachers and administrators could and should develop other questions together to address their particular local and state concerns and issues. The most important idea, of course, behind "continuing the conversation" is to promote opportunities for self-study, teacher involvement, teacher reflection, sharing of professional knowledge, and self-imposed participation in professional development. The response form included after this chapter can be photocopied and used as the focal point of a faculty discussion or a teacher study group. Teachers and schools wishing to do so are invited to make multiple copies of the form. The survey is also available on Heinemann's website: www.heinemann.com.

Your Personal Invitation to Participate

So now it is time! Teachers and other school professionals, please enter the debate! Your input is needed and requested. Respond to "the expert study" agreements and take back some of the control.

Please fill in the requested information on the survey regarding your position and experience, and then review the original total agreement lists, marking with a check all of those you agree with. Following the agreement lists, room is provided for any questions, concerns, ideas, or other comments you'd like to share. Additionally, at the end of the survey you are invited to contribute your own classroom portrait (similar in format to those presented in Chapter Four), if you wish to share. Please then mail the survey to me at the Heinemann address indicated. I am anxious to hear from all school professionals (teachers, administrators, curriculum coordinators, librarians, and other specialists). Please share your "voices" as soon as possible. The time has come!

References

Allington, R.L. and S.A. Walmsley. (1995). "No Quick Fix: Where Do We Go from Here?" In *No Quick Fix: Rethinking Literacy Programs in America's Elementary Schools*, ed. R.L. Allington and S.A. Walmsley, 253–264. New York: Teachers College Press. Newark, DE: International Reading Association.

Calfee, R. 1996. "Assessing Critical Literacy: Tools and Techniques." In *The First R: Every Child's Right to Read*, ed. M.F. Graves, P. Van den Brock and B.M. Taylor, 224–249. New York: Teachers College Press. Newark, DE: International Reading Association.

Coles, G. 1998. *Reading Lessons: The Debate over Literacy*. New York: Hill and Wang.

Elley, W. 1994. "Preface." In *The IEA Study of Reading Literacy: Achievement and Instruction in Thirty-Two School Systems*, ed. W. Elley, xxi–xxii. Oxford, England: Pergamon.

Flippo, R.F. 1997. *Reading Assessment and Instruction: A Qualitative Approach to Diagnosis*. Fort Worth, TX: Harcourt Brace College Publishers.

McQuillan, J. 1998. *The Literacy Crisis: False Claims, Real Solutions*. Portsmouth, NH: Heinemann.

Morrow, L. 1992. "The Impact of a Literature-Based Program on Literacy Achievement, Use of Literature, and Attitudes of Children from Minority Backgrounds." *Reading Research Quarterly*, 27 (3): 250–275.

Schroeder, A. 1997. *Smoky Mountain Rose.* New York: Dial Books.

Strickland, D. and B. Cullinan. 1990. "Afterword." In *Beginning to Read: Thinking and Learning About Print*, ed. M. Adams, 426–434. Cambridge, MA: MIT Press.

What Do the Experts Say?
The School Professional Survey *

Which of the following best describes your most recent position? (Check only one.)

____ Teacher

____ Reading/Language Arts Specialist

____ Curriculum Coordinator

____ Principal/Administrator

____ School Librarian/Media Specialist

____ Other School Professional

In your most recent position, which of the following grade levels did you work with? (Check only one.)

____ Pre-School   ____ Grade 5

____ Kindergarten   ____ Grade 6

____ Grade 1   ____ Early Childhood School

____ Grade 2   ____ Elementary School

____ Grade 3   ____ Middle/Junior High School

____ Grade 4   ____ High School

In your most recent position, which of the following describes the population you worked with? (Check all that apply.)

____ advantaged urban   ____ advantaged rural

____ disadvantaged urban   ____ disadvantaged rural

____ advantaged suburban   ____ Bilingual/ESL

____ disadvantaged suburban   ____ Special Education

Please write in the state/province and country in which you have most recently worked.

_____
state/province

_____
country

Total years of professional experience (Check only one.)

____ 1–2 years

____ 3–4 years

____ 5–9 years

____ 10–20 years

____ over 20 years

Highest Educational Degree (Check only one.)

____ Bachelor's

____ Master's

____ Education Specialist

____ Doctorate

* This survey is intended specifically for educators in pre-k through twelfth grade settings.

Please check *all* of the contexts and practices you agree "**Would Make Learning to Read Difficult.**" Even though some of these statements are similar or they overlap, *check each one that you agree with.*

_____ 1. Teach the children in your classroom letters and words one at a time, making sure each new letter or word is learned before moving on to the next letter or word.

_____ 2. Make word-perfect reading the prime objective of your classroom reading program.

_____ 3. Detect and correct all inappropriate or incorrect eye movements you observe as you watch children in your classroom during silent reading.

_____ 4. Emphasize only phonics instruction.

_____ 5. Make sure kids do it correctly or not at all.

_____ 6. Teach reading as something separate from writing, talking, and listening.

_____ 7. Give off expectations that reading is difficult and complex, and that "I really don't think you can do this."

_____ 8. Never let your pupils witness you enjoying/using reading.

_____ 9. Follow a basal without thinking.

_____ 10. Encourage competitive reading.

_____ 11. Use workbooks in every reading lesson.

_____ 12. Expect pupils to be able to spell all the words they can read.

_____ 13. Focus on skills rather than interpretation and comprehension.

_____ 14. If a child is not getting it, assign a few more skill sheets to remedy the problem.

_____ 15. Focus on the single best answer.

_____ 16. Make sure children understand the seriousness of falling behind.

_____ 17. Remove the freedom to make decisions about reading from the learner.

_____ 18. Group readers according to ability and let them know which group is the lowest.

_____ 19. Read infrequently to children.

_____ 20. Select all the stories children can read.

_____ 21. Stop reading aloud to children as soon as they get through the primer level.

_____ 22. Follow a basal series without questioning or reflecting on what you are doing.

_____ 23. Have kids read short, snappy texts rather than whole stories.

_____ 24. Make word-perfect oral reading the prime objective of your classroom reading program.

_____ 25. Have the children do oral reading exclusively.

_____ 26. In small groups, have children orally read a story, allowing one sentence or paragraph at a time for each child, and going around the group in either a clockwise or counter-clockwise rotation.

_____ 27. Drill children extensively on isolated letters and sounds using flashcards, the blackboard, or worksheets.

_____ 28. Test children with paper and pencil tests every time they complete a new story in their basal, and every time you have finished teaching a new skill.

_____ 29. Never give children books in which some of the words are unknown (i.e., words that you haven't previously taught or exposed them to in some way).

_____ 30. Be sure that you provide lots of training on all the reading skills prior to letting children read a story silently. Even if there isn't much time left for actual reading, you have to focus first on skill training.

_____ 31. Reading correctly or pronouncing words "exactly right" should be a prime objective of your classroom reading program.

_____ 32. Require children to write book reviews of every book they read.

_____ 33. Use flashcards to drill on isolated letter sounds.

Please check _all_ of the contexts and practices that **"Would Facilitate Learning to Read."** Even though some of these statements are similar or they overlap, _check each one that you agree with._

_____ 1. Develop positive self-perceptions and expectations.

_____ 2. Use every opportunity to bring reading/writing/talking/listening together so that each feeds off and feeds into the other.

_____ 3. Provide multiple, repeated demonstrations of how reading is done and/or used.

_____ 4. Organize your classroom around a variety of print settings, and use a variety of print settings in your classroom.

_____ 5. Focus on using reading as a tool for learning.

_____ 6. Use a broad spectrum of sources for student reading materials (i.e., children's literature, newspapers, magazines, etc.).

_____ 7. Combine reading and writing.

_____ 8. Make reading functional.

_____ 9. Include a variety of printed material and literature in your classroom so that students are exposed to numerous types of printed materials (i.e., newspapers, magazines, journals, textbooks, research books, trade books, library books, etc.).

_____ 10. Give your students lots of time and opportunity to read real books. Likewise, give your students lots of time and opportunity to write creatively and/or for purposeful school assignments.

_____ 11. Plan instruction and individual work so students engage in purposeful reading and writing most of the time rather than consciously separating reading from writing activities.

_____ 12. Create environments, contexts in which the children become convinced that reading does further the purposes of their lives.

_____ 13. Encourage children to talk about and share the different kinds of reading they do in a variety of ways with many others.

_____ 14. Use a range of functions of reading (print in the environment, magazines, newspapers, menus, directions, etc.).

_____ 15. Use silent reading whenever appropriate to the specific purpose.

Questions, concerns, ideas, or other comments you would like to share:

Do you have a classroom portrait (similar in format to one of those presented in Chapter Four) that you would like to share? If so, please attach and sign/date it (also include your mailing address), indicating your permission to publish without remuneration an edited/modified version in a future report of this follow-up study. Also, indicate if you give permission to use your name (if so, print carefully), or whether you prefer a pseudonym, if your portrait is selected.

Thank you for participating and sharing your expertise in this follow-up study. Please send your response pages to me at Heinemann.

Rona Flippo
c/o Heinemann
Promotions Department
361 Hanover Street
Portsmouth, New Hampshire 03801–3912

About the Contributing Teachers

Gay Fawcett taught kindergarten for six years, first grade for five years, and third grade for two years. She then served four years as the Language Arts Consultant for the Summit County Educational Service Center in Ohio. She is currently the Director of Curriculum and Instruction for the Center. Gay has been one of the associate editors of *The Reading Teacher* journal, published by International Reading Association.

Lilia Del Carmen Monzó is a bilingual teacher in Los Angeles. She has worked primarily with low-income Latino and Chicano communities throughout some of California's inner cities. She has taught grades one, three, and four. She is also taking graduate courses at the University of Southern California.

Kim Boothroyd taught pre-k and first grade in Seattle, Washington. She then taught second and fourth grade in central New York for a number of years. Later, Kim was the reading coordinator at an independent school in New York City for five years. She is currently taking graduate courses in reading and writing instruction at the University of New Hampshire.

Margaret Berry taught first grade for four years and now teaches second grade at the University School of Nashville in Nashville, Tennessee. She holds a Masters of Education degree from Peabody College at Vanderbilt University. Prior to becoming a teacher, she practiced law for six years with a private law firm in Nashville.

About the Author

Rona Flippo has taught and directed a pre-school program, and has taught second and third grade in several schools in Florida and in South Carolina. She has also served as an inservice reading teacher for a public middle school; a consultant for Educational Testing Service and for the Georgia Department of Education; and a reading professor at various colleges and universities in Florida, South Carolina, Georgia, Wisconsin, and most recently, Massachusetts.

Rona is currently Professor of Reading Education at Fitchburg State College in Massachusetts, where she teaches both undergraduate and graduate students. She has previously published six books and over eighty articles, chapters, reviews, editorials, and other publications. Most recently, she authored *Reading Assessment and Instruction: A Qualitative Approach to Diagnosis* (Harcourt Brace College Publishers, 1997) and she also has several other books "in press" or under development.

Rona is an active member and participant of the International Reading Association and the National Reading Conference; in both organizations, Rona serves on key committees. Additionally, she has served on many editorial boards for various journals concerned with reading.